A *quiet word* with your horse

Marlitt Wendt

A *quiet word*
with your horse

Learning by reward –
The key to motivation and trust

CADMOS

Imprint

Copyright@ 2012 Cadmos Publishing Limited, Richmond, UK
Copyright of the original edition ©2011 by Cadmos Verlag,
Schwarzenbek

Design: Ravenstein + Partner, Verden
Setting: Das Agenturhaus, Munich
Editor of the original edition: Anneke Bosse
Editor of this edition: Christopher Long
Printed by: Grafisches Centrum Cuno, Calbe

Cover photo: Stephen Rasche-Hilpert
Content photos: Cornelia Ranz
Translation: Claire Williams

Printed by: Grafisches Centrum Cuno, Calbe

British Library Cataloguing in Publication Data
A catalogue record of this book is available from the
British Library

Printed in Germany

ISBN 978-0-85788-007-9

CONTENTS

A *quiet word* with your horse

CONTENTS

A *quiet word* with your horse

Foreword: beginning a dialogue

Many horse lovers spend the majority of their free time with their horses. The relationship that develops out of this is like a dance, a two-way communication between you and your four-legged partner, which is fed into by the empathy that you have for your horse's feelings and an understanding of how it moves. When training horses it is essential to choose a method that is suited to both human and horse, so that as well as the dance steps you learn the essence of the dancing style. When the first basic steps and the background to the dance have been mastered, you can think about adding steps and combinations, or even advanced movements or improvisation, just as in dancing.

The basis for training horses positively is the horse's own learning behaviour and psyche. Only a person who understands why and how a horse behaves and thinks can truly open a dialogue with one. It is only then that we can start to work on our own dancing ability and start to refine our own technique.

The exercises introduced in this book are practical examples of what a training programme may look like. The emphasis is on the word "may", because of course every single part of training must be tailored to the ability of the individual horse. There is no guaranteed method and it is only through empathy and an understanding of the way a horse's mind works that we can achieve success together.

Our pursuit of technical perfection all too often distracts us from what is actually important on a daily basis – the joy of working together and the emotional balance of horse and rider. Whether on the dance floor or in the arena, a contented way of going and an expression of inner balance are the rewards for horse and rider of treating each other with respect. Given that every person and every horse is different, you must find out for yourself the form that your own personal dialogue needs to take to communicate with your horse.

Marlitt Wendt, August 2011

There is another way – a question of feeling

Why do so many riders invest their valuable free time carrying out boring exercises with their horses, and then complain about how badly their horses are going? They often resort to the more forceful means demanded by many of the traditional methods of training, while at the same time feeling anything but happy. Isn't this rather different from how we imagined riding would be? We wanted to have fun, enjoy the great outdoors with our horses, be free from worry and really become one with our horse. What, more often than not, is left of this dream? Nothing but a feeling of wanting to achieve more than you can, of not being good enough, made worse by social pressure placed on you by others in your yard. In other words you become frustrated. Does it really have to be like this? Can you really train horses only by methods that use force and pressure? I can assure you that this is not the case. The training of horses and the time we spend together with these wonderful creatures doesn't need to be like this. There is another way.

You and your horse will learn best in a relaxed atmosphere.

What happened to just having fun?

It's a self-fulfilling prophecy that riding and training horses leads to work. We know this from many of the common things we do, such as ground work, training in-hand and riding lessons. The time we spend with our horses tends to be characterised by an atmosphere of hard work and we have a clear idea in our minds of what we have to achieve. At the same time, though, work is often perceived as something that is far from being fun.

Given that the work we are doing involves learning certain movements or is designed to train our horses and make them supple, it can't possibly also be fun for either horse or rider. Or can it? Does it really have to be like this?

Think back to a time in your life when you were relaxed and having fun, such as when you were on a particularly enjoyable holiday. You are likely to be able to remember lots of minute details, such as the sea glinting in the distance, the exotic smells and the different types of food you ate. In retrospect the holiday will appear to be much longer than perhaps it really was; the days will be filled with different activities and lots of apparently insignificant details, all of which will have been burned firmly into your memory. This is precisely because you don't feel as though you actually had to learn or remember anything. Learning, and with it the memory of the smallest detail, was in effect a by-product of the experience. They fact that you can remember so much occurred totally accidentally, without you being aware of it or even desiring it.

Just as we can save memories of good experiences quite accidentally, our horses can learn through enjoyment, and be happy when doing so. To do this we must rid ourselves of the notion of wanting to teach horses something. This transition from being superior, a teacher, to taking a more equal position of learning together brings with it a change in perspective. Remember that horses are perfect just the way they are; we have to learn to make ourselves understood and teach ourselves how to communicate with them. Every training method is based on certain assumptions, and on a specific belief system upon which the followers of the method have agreed. People often talk at cross purposes – one person might assume that the Earth is flat, with the Sun and the stars revolving above it, while the other sees the Earth as round with the Sun circling around

Training can also be done without pressure.

it. Their views of the world and the reality that they portray are fundamentally different, but each believes that their view is the most valid one.

In most of the current training methods, the underlying belief system is based on the assumption that the horse has to be taught specific things, and that this teaching has something to do with a relationship that involves dominance, in the form of a hierarchy. The horse is taught to react to the deliberate application and release of pressure. The horse has to submit itself unconditionally to the demands of its rider, and self-initiative is not encouraged. If we, as riders, don't feel comfortable within this belief system, perhaps because it doesn't reflect our own ideas and we don't want to or can't identify with the way horses are treated as a result, then we will not gain any real enjoyment from our horses.

In general, traditions have left their mark on equestrianism, as have the personal observations and opinions of many well-known horsemen and women. The method of training horses introduced in this book is based less on tradition and more on scientific knowledge of the psychology of learning and the basics of behavioural science. For this reason I will be assuming the following definitions and theories, which come from the scientific study of animal behaviour (ethology), and which I will clarify and explain throughout the book.

- Horses learn constantly and they do so from every situation.

- There is no such thing as non-communication.
- Learning is an individual process and has nothing to do with hierarchy.
- Signals are not orders.
- People are not essentially brighter than horses, but they just have a different type of intelligence.
- You can train without using pressure.

Every belief system will have its own specific effect on the psyche of the person who follows it. If we view our horse as a working animal, such as in the cowboy tradition, it will be difficult for us to build play into our training rather than putting absolute obedience to the fore. An alternative vision of training would be to concentrate on the "we", and to put the horse's enjoyment to the fore by allowing it to volunteer its work. In the case of "we" it is the feeling of mutual understanding that will fill both horse and human with enthusiasm, and our horses will reward us with increased levels of attention and their open curiosity for what will become a mutual hobby.

A horse's rights

Every rider and horse lover should think about what the natural rights of a horse actually are. Under our animal welfare laws, every animal has the right to be kept in a way that is appropriate for its species. This includes being fed and housed appropriately, and in my opinion a horse also has the right to be treated and trained in a humane

Every horse has the right to be treated and kept in a way that is fair and appropriate.

and ethically correct manner. You should, whenever possible, try to achieve your training goals without the use of methods that involve pressure or physical force. Remember that psychological pressure is a form of force that should not be underestimated. Aids or signals given by a rider are not orders, but rather requests made of the horse. Given that you are entering into a dialogue with your horse, it should be given the opportunity to comment and have its viewpoint considered. Of course there will be times when we have to be able to control a horse's behaviour in order not to endanger others, but this should not be the sole

basis for training, as is often taught. Therefore you must differentiate between training sessions during which the horse is given the opportunity to learn without fear of pressure or punishment and those that have to involve exceptions to this rule.

Follow your own dream

It is sometimes difficult to change the way things are done when you are part of a social system that is as influenced by tradition as the equestrian

15

Live the same dream together.

world. There are firm views and opinions like: "We have always done it like that", or even "If you don't make it do it then your horse will walk all over you". If you attempt to break out of this straitjacket of expectations, even slightly, then you could be quickly shunned – at best you will be avoided or made fun of, at worst you may face open hostility. However, to achieve your and your horse's happiness there is no other option than to follow your own dream of how you imagine your time together can be. Would you like to be treated the same way as a horse often is during a riding lesson? If not, then the question has to be asked whether you can ever be truly happy with the traditional

way in which riding is taught and horses are trained. If we take advantage of our own human right to live our life the way we feel we should be able to, then the time we spend with our horses should also be one in which can do as we wish and find enjoyment.

In self-contemplation

There is naturally a long process of learning, observing and gathering experience before you reach a stage at which you are completely at ease working and being with your horse. Both horses and people are complex living beings; to understand them requires a certain level of knowledge and practice. Once you are comfortable being around and working with your horse, you will need to tackle the idea of establishing a goal-orientated system of training. Only those who follow a plan and understand what this plan consists of will ever achieve what they want to in terms of training their horses. In this respect, every training method is only as good as the trainer. The positive training system that I introduce here is a complex method and one that has to be studied in order for it to be successful. Although the foundation of positive horse training lies in taking a playful approach and creating a relaxed training atmosphere, this apparent lightness in approach should never be confused with inconsistency or laxness, or even an anti-authoritarian teaching process. When you are trying to establish a new form of communication with your horse, a high degree of consistency and self-analysis is required, together with a well-structured training programme. In addition, knowledge of how learning occurs and the behavioural patterns of both horse and human is crucial. This new philosophy of working together and respecting your horse demands a high level of concentration and consistency from all of those involved; in return you will gain a fascinating insight into how your four-legged partners see the world and into their mental capacity, which may so far have been unknown to you. If you are prepared to really open yourself up to carrying out a serious dialogue with your horse this unconventional partnership will offer you many new experiences and enjoyable moments.

Before you can enter into a dialogue, you must agree on the language to be spoken.

Positive horse training –

the potential for learning by reward

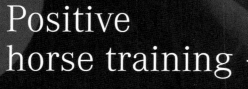

Communication occurs whenever you have contact with your horse. Information or signs given through body language are exchanged, which have to be interpreted or learned by both partners. It is of crucial importance therefore that you take a closer look specifically at horses' learning behaviour. A horse's brain operates different learning processes that can be running constantly in parallel to one another. Learning can't be switched on and off at will during a training session but instead takes place constantly, even when the horse is sleeping. For this reason you have to be very aware of what information you are communicating to your horse, because it will be drawing conclusions from your behaviour all the time. The different ways in which a horse learns can be used with varying degrees of success when you are training your horse; imagine that they are like different kinds of channels through which a horse receives and interprets pictures. During this process, the horse's emotional connection to the learning and training outcomes is of great significance. If a horse feels happy around us and receives confirmation and a feeling of achievement then it will find it easier to learn and will have a longer lasting memory of its behaviour.

Only if it is made worth doing will the horse respond to your command to come to you.

situations. Through its senses, every living being is in constant contact with the world around it, so that the process of learning is also taking place perpetually. In terms of the learning behaviour of horses, this continuous processing of information means in principle that they are always exhibiting behaviour, in effect they are constantly reacting to their environment, and that it is impossible for them, as it is with humans, to show a form of non-behaviour or impassiveness. In the same way, horses and humans are communicating continually, with the result that we can't just take a break in our communication when working together.

In the process of conditioning, the horse learns from the results of its own behaviour. Behaviour that is rewarded or made worthwhile will in the future be exhibited more often. On the other hand, a type of behaviour that is not rewarded will be carried out less frequently. This doesn't just apply to behaviour that may be shown currently, but also to that displayed some time ago. Horses will repeat behaviour that may have been rewarded at some time in the past. This is one of the reasons why, for example, a horse may start begging for food, even when doing so has worked only once in the past.

Learning as a process

The process of learning serves to adjust behaviour to the environmental conditions and to adapt physical reactions to changing

Four ways to control behaviour

To influence a horse's behaviour and to train it, there are in principle four ways of having an effect on the conditioning process.

1. You can do something to the horse that it finds unpleasant, for example exerting pressure in the hope that the horse will change its behaviour.

2. You can stop doing something that the horse finds unpleasant, such as releasing pressure when the horse does what you want.

3. You can give the animal something that it likes, as a reward for doing an exercise correctly.

4. You can stop doing something that the horse likes, withdrawing a reward such as scratching its neck.

The key to motivation

For horses to show certain behaviour voluntarily, they have to be appropriately motivated to do so – in other words they need to have an inner willingness to carry out the action. By working with rewards, or positive reinforcement as it is also called, the horse is more motivated to do something together with you. Horses become more active and will work with you when, in the true sense of the term, it is worth their while to do so. Just as we go to work for material (or even immaterial) gains such as a salary, horses also want to see some results for their efforts.

Rewards-based learning stimulates horses' intelligence and their connection to the people around them.

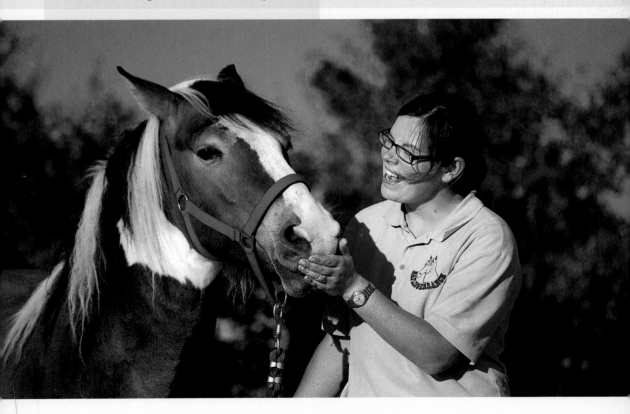

A game of chase can also serve as a reward.

Rewards are most effective when they satisfy one of a horse's essential needs, such as hunger or some other appetite, human affection, or just something that the horse will enjoy. There are therefore a variety of different types of reward that can be used when training horses, depending on the particular preferences of the individual horse. For some horses tit-bits are like heaven on earth whilst others yearn more for a gentle rub or a quick game of chase. Once we have found this out, we can use different primary reinforcers or rewards, depending on the situation. Starting to play a game together would not be practical form of reward to use when riding. In this case it would be more sensible to use a tit-bit or a gentle rub as a reward.

Rewards can be rewarding

Horses can best relate a certain action or behaviour to a reward when it is given at virtually the same time as the behaviour is shown. In standardised experiments, behavioural researchers discovered that you only have up to three seconds to give the horse its reward. In practice, when you are training surrounded by a normal level of distraction, this time is reduced to one or two seconds at most. Horses learn quickest of all when (re)action and reward occur at exactly the same time. If you don't time it right then the horse may learn something totally different from what you are actually trying to teach.

Here is an example that involves the mistiming of a reward. I am standing with my horse tied up to a ring on the wall and would like it to move over so that I can get to its other side more easily. I give it the cue or signal to move over, one that it has already learnt, such as a touch on its flank. My horse moves over as asked. I would now like to reward it with a tit-bit because it has been so good, and I start to dig about in my jacket pocket. My horse starts to paw the ground impatiently and I give it its treat. What has it now learnt and what have I actually just rewarded? It is likely that the horse will no longer associate the perfect turn on the forehand with the treat, because the process of digging around in my pockets and presenting the treat to the horse lasted longer than three seconds. The horse will associate the reward instead with what it was doing at the moment the treat was offered, namely the more undesirable action of pawing the ground. It will now do this more frequently because, from the horse's perspective, it was this action that was rewarded. I have therefore reinforced the wrong behaviour because I wasn't careful enough to make the reward coincide with the desired action.

Effective training requires precisely timed rewards.

With a clicker we can clearly mark desirable behaviour.

Apparently the same – but very different

The precise moment at which the tit-bit or similar reward is given to a horse is therefore of crucial significance. However, it is quite simple to get around the problem of rewarding too late, which can occur when we are working at some distance from the horse, for example when lungeing, by introducing our horse to a more general system of reward. We need to agree on a positive common language, a motivating "Yes-language". The first step towards this common tongue begins when a horse learns that a specific noise is always made when we want to tell them that they have done something right and can expect a reward. This noise therefore indicates the type of behaviour that the horse should show more often, and shows that it is heading in the right direction in its learning. In practice it is totally irrelevant from the horse's point of view what noise is made, but before beginning its training this noise should not have had any significance or meaning to the horse – in other words it needs to be as neutral a tone as possible. In general training, the unmistakable sound of the clicker has proven its own worth. A clicker is a small plastic box with a metal strip that makes a sharp clicking sound when pushed and released. However, the horse does have to get used to the sound before the training actually starts so that it can learn its significance. To be suitable for use as an audible reward in training, the sound has to be reproducible, and it should be easy to differentiate from the human voice. Here the advantage of the clicker becomes obvious because it produces a clearly recognisable noise that stands out from human speech. It can also be heard over longer distances, because it falls into a frequency range that is particularly easy for a horse to hear.

Use of this basic process of conditioning in training our horse means that it learns that a physical reward always follows the audible reward. This conditioning allows us to tell the horse, even when we are not standing directly in front of the horse with a treat at the ready, that it has done something correctly. This gives us more time to give a feed reward. In the example given above we would use the clicker as the horse moved over and could shortly thereafter provide it with its tit-bit. The prerequisite for this is that the horse has already undergone conditioning so that it understands the meaning of the clicker. It will then understand that it has received the treat just because it moved over. Clicker training, or training with sound as a reward, makes it possible to give a precise indication of when desirable behaviour occurs, which is a prerequisite for effective communication and a successful training programme. The click becomes the secondary reinforcement in the conditioning process, in other words it is a reinforcer that indicates that the primary reward, the edible treat, is about to follow.

The reward follows the click

The exercise that is about to be described is fundamental to your training. It is indispensable, and is a prerequisite for many of the exercises that will follow. It should therefore be given particular time and attention. In the process of operant conditioning the horse learns by trial and error that

During initial conditioning, every time the cone touches the horse it is marked with a click. Alex then has up to two seconds to give her horse its tit-bit.

it has first of all to complete a simple task, after which the chosen tone will be heard, followed by the actual reward. This is how the horse learns the sentence structure of your new common language. As a first step the horse has to learn the significance of the clicker, which will later act as the marker signal.

For this initial conditioning, apart from the clicker itself, you will need a supply of appropriate bite-sized treats in an accessible bag that you can easily get your hand in and out of, as well as a place that is both quiet and safe for you and your horse, such as a indoor or outdoor school. You will also need an object that is eye-catching but sturdy and robust, such as a fly swat, small cone or even a frisbee, that will act as your target.

Once you have taken up position with the target and clicker in one hand and your horse alongside you, wait for your horse to touch the object that you have brought with you, whether out of curiosity or by accident. As soon as even a whisker comes into contact with the object press the clicker and push a treat into your horse's mouth with your other hand, ideally at exactly the same time. Once the horse has eaten the treat, it will hopefully want to examine and then touch the object again. Click and reward in exactly the same way again and repeat this ten to fifteen times. Take a five minute break by removing the object from the horse's sight.

Follow this at another time with a similar session of touch–click–reward. You will notice very quickly that your horse begins to understand the connection. It will intentionally touch its nose to the target, prick its ears towards the source of the noise and look for its treat.

At this stage you can slowly start to change the position of the target by holding it lower down or further away from the horse's head so that it has to stretch in order to reach it. It is very important that the horse's efforts are always rewarded with a click and a treat.

You should resist the temptation, however, to move the target towards the horse's muzzle. Always wait patiently until the horse actively makes contact with the unaccustomed object. Only then will it start to recognise clicker training as a voluntary form of training in which we are looking for initiative and creativity.

Has the penny dropped?

Even just this first session will have "clicked" with many horses in more ways than one. To check that the penny has dropped for your horse, and that it now recognises the click as a marker of its own behaviour and as a cue that a treat is about to come, carry out a small comprehension test. After your horse has touched the target, click as you would normally but then wait for a few seconds with the treat in your hand and watch your horse. If your horse has understood that it should always receive a treat after the click it will move its head towards your hand to look for the treat, which you should then quickly give it.

Aren't I clever?

As a further training session try a second comprehension test. Hide the target so the horse can't see it and wait for the horse to turn its attention onto something else thinking that the game is over. If it starts to turn away from you, click once. The horse is likely to be surprised because you have changed the structure of the game but if it has really understood the significance of the clicker, it should turn towards you and, possibly because of the build-up of saliva and anticipation, start to chew. This is a sure sign that it has learnt the most important vocabulary of its newly acquired language, namely that the click is directly connected to food. Once you have reached this level of understanding you can truly begin to communicate with your horse and expand your vocabulary bit by bit.

A training session should always finish on a note of success, so make sure you finish the initial conditioning exercise by repeating what has already been understood, the sequence of touch-click-reward. Given that horses can really

Understanding without words.

only concentrate for a few minutes at a time this initial conditioning should consist of a series of short units that last only a few minutes each.

When understanding dawns

During the conditioning process a special moment will occur in the relationship with your horse, which is the magical moment of comprehension. This is the stage at which the light of understanding will dawn in your horse and you will become witness to something very moving. You can actually see your horse thinking. The first time the horse touches the target is likely to be by chance, but very soon you will see a change in the animal. It will become more aware of its actions and will, bit by bit, begin to touch the target almost with excessive care as if to say "Look what I can do, can you understand me?". Your horse will make contact with you by using its ears and eyes almost as if to reassure itself that you are really communicating.

It is a moment of mutual understanding that is also mirrored in the horse's body language and expression. It will appear suddenly to be totally awake, in the here and now, and will have a soft expression in its eyes. The horse's twitching ears and mobile upper lip will show its enjoyment. The brightness of its eyes will be like that of a child getting its presents on Christmas Day. Some horse owners have told me that at this moment they felt for the first time that their horse had truly understood them and that they had really looked them in the eye. It is one of those rare moments of mutual

A deeper relationship will only come from a sense of understanding.

understanding. You are building the first bridge of understanding and are entering into a real dialogue with your very different conversational partner.

Have a go, it's worth it!

For very cautious or timid horses, the task of touching a strange object can be too much. In this case don't wait for the horse to make the first move, but just click regardless of what the horse does. It can even just simply stand there and look at the surroundings. It is important that you click and immediately offer a tit-bit several times. An exception to this would of course be if the horse was displaying undesirable behaviour such as pawing the ground. Turn away until it stops doing what you don't want it to do and click exactly at the moment when it stands still.

After this initial session try the comprehension test described above to see whether your horse has started to understand the significance of the clicker.

This sequence should be followed for the next two or three days, preferably repeated several times a day so that the association click = food is established. Only then should you move on to more demanding techniques of operant conditioning if you have a passive or timid horse.

Even those of a more timid nature can be successful quickly once they have understood the link between a click and a reward.

From chaos to order –
training theory

Effective training always requires a certain amount of knowledge and preparation before starting, but what is decisive is your own attitude towards your horse and the method of training that you choose. The valuable spare time that you spend with your horse shouldn't be marred by unrealistic expectations. Instead, simply learning a new way of communicating can be a continual source of real enjoyment for the partnership of horse and rider. Every single day the inner relationship you have with your horse will be strengthened as the understanding you have of your four-legged partner's intellectual potential grows. As well as the insight into the specific learning behaviour of horses already mentioned, you should also take into account various aspects of training theory when developing your plan. Only a person who builds up a sensible and structured training plan and sets realistic goals, without asking too much of themselves or their horse, whilst at the same time taking into account certain basic rules of the game, will be able to see their dream of being able to communicate with their horse come true.

On an emotional rollercoaster

Training of both horse and handler always goes particularly well and proceeds without stress when we start the session well prepared and organised. This includes ensuring that the right conditions are present

The emotional balance between the partners determines the success of a training session.

and that you have an array of games to play that you can use to best advantage. The most decisive teaching tool however is your own positive attitude towards your partner. If we are not true to ourselves it can have a negative effect on the course of a training session. It is sensible to put your everyday worries to one side before heading off to visit your horse, or at least do something to reduce your own stress levels so that you are relaxed when you come into contact with your horse.

Strong emotions on both sides can not only affect the mood during your work together but also the memory afterwards of what has been learnt. A horse will always show a different expression during a lesson that is carried out with a degree of stress involved, compared with one that was done calmly and with more harmony. Given that horses react extremely sensitively to those around them, it is important to be very aware of your own mood. It is better to miss a day's training if you are not feeling right, choosing instead just to play with your horse or enjoy its company. Horses aren't emotional rubbish bins, nor are they responsible for easing our tensions, and they are certainly not responsible for whether we are feeling successful or in a good mood.

Correctly equipped for action?

Besides the clicker, the most important aids for use with a positive training method are treats that your horse really likes eating, a variety of indestructible toys for rewarding with play, one or more belt- or waist-bags to store your edible treats in, and a bag for treats that can be attached to your saddle. A well-fenced and preferably quiet area to work in, and tack that fits the horse properly, complete the picture. In this initial phase a halter and lead rope, and later a saddle, are important.

The ideal bag for treats is one that is robust and large enough that you can get your hand in and out of it easily. It is also useful for it to have a zip or drawstring closure so that you don't lose half the treats while you are working. During the initial training and work in-hand, conventional belt- or bum-bags will do the job, or you could try a so-called "bait bag". These are used in dog training and should be available from your pet store. When riding it is better to use saddle bags or something similar that can be attached to the front of the saddle so the rider's mobility isn't restricted.

Why do I need a bag for the treats? Why can't I just put them in my pockets? You can do this, but when you are a beginner this can cause unnecessary distractions. You can't reach into a pocket as easily and you will have to fill them up a lot more often than you would a bag, especially at the start when you need a lot of treats.

The bag for treats is the most important piece of equipment in positive horse training. It should be roomy and easy to wear.

Mental preparation

Your training plan should give you a series of pictures in your mind that show what you want to achieve as your goal. In addition you should think of as many small goals along the way as you can, which will help to divide up the lessons into easily digestible portions. It is important to be clear at every step how you are going to get to the next one. It is not as easy as it might appear to divide up a desired behavioural pattern or movement into its component parts. As an example, the Spanish walk can't just be reduced to

Seeing pictures in your mind can help you to divide your training goals into individual steps.

the lifting and stretching of a foreleg. Work has also to be done on the stepping up and through of the hind legs, while keeping a careful eye on the horse's collected outline so that you can see whether the horse is likely to perform the movement correctly from the first muscle contraction on, and then reward it appropriately.

Horses can only concentrate for a short amount of time so effective training should only ever be carried out in brief but intensive sessions. Of course, fully grown horses can go for an hour-long ride or a longer hack. However, concentrated phases of learning, during which something new is being taught or something already learnt is being cemented, should only ever last for a few minutes. During each exercise the learning process of every horse follows a typical learning curve. Learning is not a process that shows a steady rise and improvement, but is a rather dynamic occurrence.

It is quite normal for learning sometimes to happen faster, sometimes slower, and then to stagnate on reaching a certain level. These plateaus in learning, during which nothing seems to happen, are however immensely important for the horse's brain. Every horse lover must allow their horse the opportunity to consolidate behaviour at a certain level, because only then will there be a new jump in the learning curve. Sometimes it might appear that a horse takes a massive step in improvement overnight. Horses really do learn during breaks in training as well as when they are asleep, as they process their experiences subconsciously. The tempo at which a horse learns is totally dependent on the individual horse. It is normal for one lesson to be easier for horse A while horse B shows its true potential in a different exercise. Just as with humans, horses are individuals with their own preferences and natural abilities. Learning plateaus are no reason for worry, but on the contrary are a reason to be happy, because you are usually just about to see a breakthrough, as long as you don't destroy the chance by being too ambitious.

The rules of the game for handlers

During the training process, performance of the desired behaviour at the appropriate level is marked immediately, or within two seconds, by our conditioned secondary reinforcement. From this it follows that every click or other audible

A horse can only be well trained if the handler really understands the philosophy behind the training and knows how to apply it.

reward has to occur ideally at the same time as the behaviour is exhibited. Therefore one of the most important rules for the handler is to maintain absolute concentration on the horse and what is happening. Every glance around, every time you chat with someone else and every time you let your thoughts drift will delay the training process because you may miss subtle signs of progress from your horse or won't be in a position to mark them clearly.

A good scratch can for some horses be reward enough, as the ecstatic expression here shows.

The audible reward or click is not a command by itself. It simply marks a desired action and means, translated into our language, something like, "Yes, that's right!" This means that a click should never be used to attract a horse's attention. To give you an example – my horse runs away from me in the field. I can't be bothered to run after it and use the clicker because I know that my horse will stand still when it hears it because it is expecting a treat. I am using the click as a command in the sense of "Stand still!" This might well work once or twice, but what is the horse learning? It is learning to do more of exactly what it was doing when it heard the click – namely running away. You are unintentionally teaching the horse the game of "I'll run away so that I get a treat". This is not what you wanted to do at all. Therefore, you should only mark and reward desirable behaviour. In clicker training there is a very appropriate saying: "What you click is what you get". It is always the handler, with inappropriate reward behaviour, that causes the wrong behaviour in their horse. A horse can only be trained as well as its handler has understood the philosophy behind the training and can implement it.

Every click is followed inevitably by a reward. The click is a promise that you must never break, as to do so would be to deprive you of one of your own aids. If the horse finds that the click is not a one hundred percent guarantee that a reward of feed follows, a degree of uncertainty will enter the training session. The horse has to understand the conditions under which it is expected to enter into the game of training. It is the same for us – we want to know from our future employer before we start a job that we are going to receive our salary regularly and not have it put on hold arbitrarily for three months. We should spare our horses the same uncertainty. It follows logically that we should never click when we don't have a reward with us. When we recognise that a certain behaviour has been well learnt and we would like to reward it less, we can click less often in order to reduce the level of reward that needs to be handed out.

The act of giving

The reward that we choose must also be seen by the animal as a real reward. Every horse is different – what one likes another might finding boring. For us the most commonly acceptable form of payment is money, while the majority of horses are prepared to work for carrots, apples or a pat. Your priority is to find out what payment for what effort your horse sees as appropriate. No horse is likely to be prepared to perform a piaffe for some hay. The observant teacher will quickly find out what the appropriate "currency" is when working with their horse.

In the case of rewarding with feed, the individual treats used should be as small as possible. Studies have shown that a large reward does not guarantee a large step forward in progress. The act of giving, and the genuine feeling that lies behind it in willingly giving the horse something to reward its effort, is the important factor. In addition, horses become satiated quickly and will lose their appetite if after every small achievement they are rewarded with something as large as an apple. Apart from this, it takes the horse a relatively long time to eat a whole apple. Small tit-bits such as chunks of apple or a few oat grains that can be swallowed after one chew are known to work well. Most of the commercially manufactured treats are much too large and should be chopped up.

Stop when things are at their best

Depending on the ability of the horse and handler to concentrate, each unit should only last a few minutes. Regular breaks should be made a part of each unit, and every session must end on a good note. A horse will remember the end of a session particularly well, and it will remember the last seconds of training with specific intensity. If it has made a jump up the learning curve at this point it will store this piece of progress in its mind. For this reason it is important that you stop when things are going well, because after this it often only gets worse. If you are so excited by what your horse has done that you want to try, for example, the newly learned flying change for a second or third time remember that, at this stage, it is unlikely to get any better. It is preferable to try something different and to go back to the newly learned exercise the next day.

Within an exercise you should only work on one detail of behaviour at a time. If you are practising shoulder-in and are concentrating on the way the horse is stepping through from behind, you can't at the same time work on the angle or the way the legs are crossing over. You have to decide what you are going to focus on and in doing so gradually increase the difficulty of what you are asking so that the animal has a realistic chance of being rewarded. A horse will understandably get frustrated if, after learning to do a walk pirouette, it only gets rewarded again when it has learned to do it in canter.

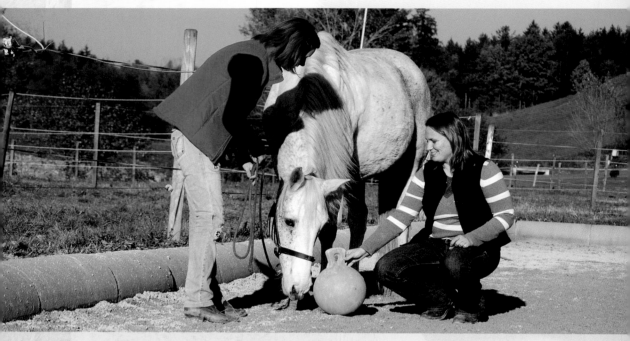

Brief but intensive training sessions bring the fastest success.

Another clicker training saying is: "Be a splitter not a lumper". In other words, break up every action into small parts so that each can be rewarded and don't lump it all together as one. When you are working on a specific detail of an exercise the other components of the end result will fade temporarily into the background. A horse might carry out a few shoulder-in steps at too great an angle if you are working on the way it is stepping through from behind. It is only when you have practised both points individually and the horse has understood them that you can combine the individual parts again.

Once a certain behaviour or action has been learned thoroughly you can move gradually from giving constant rewards to only the occasional treat for performing that exercise. However, many trainers assume too early that a horse has mastered a lesson. Think back to your own time at school. How often did you have to practise a difficult bit of vocabulary to be able to use it and really understand it in every context? Horses often lose their confidence and become insecure if something new that has been learned is not repeated often enough. Only when a horse has performed a task correctly eight times out of ten can you move from constant to occasional rewards. Before this stage the handler must mark and reward the horse every, and I mean every, time that it completes the action correctly at the current level of training. Only when you reach the stage at which a task doesn't have to be constantly rewarded can you start to move on to connecting different exercises with each other.

One of the crucial principles of training is that you must always going back to basics if, for example, the horse suddenly won't perform a task that you know it knows how to do and is capable of

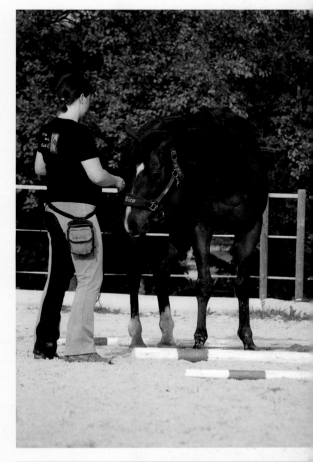

Exercises should always be broken down into component parts. In this case the horse should be rewarded for stepping over each individual pole, before it is later asked to go over all of them for just one click and reward.

doing. If a horse doesn't quite understand one of the stages in its work and you are running the risk of getting stuck at a particular point, you should ask less and go back to a part of the exercise that the horse can do well. What might appear to be a backwards step will often actually prove to be a step forwards and will avoid both the handler and the horse becoming frustrated.

The rules of the game for horses

"You're fine, just the way you are." It is only when you can transmit this feeling to your horse through your actions that it will be able to develop its potential fully and not just go through the motions of an exercise. It will perform the task with enjoyment and expression.

"It's alright to make mistakes and you don't need to worry about being punished for them." It is natural that a student will make mistakes when they are learning. Mistakes are an inescapable part of learning and they provide an opportunity to gain in experience and to learn from them. When a horse feels as if it is being treated like a subordinate and being put under pressure during a lesson, it won't be capable of showing its creative learning potential.

Understanding secondary reinforcement is an important fundamental skill for a horse. Before the start of proper training every horse must have digested and understood the principle that an audible reward (the noise that you make) marks the desired behaviour or task and signals that a much desired tit-bit is going to follow. The rewards therefore need to be earned by the

Back to basics. If something doesn't go quite how you would like it to, start again with an exercise that you know your horse can do well such as standing still on command.

Horses need to feel that we respect them and that they are seen as individuals, with their own personalities.

ly and therefore periods of concentration should be broken up with periods of relaxation or some other diversion. The frequency and length of the breaks that are required will depend on the nature and personality of each individual. Taking a break for a couple of minutes every few minutes has been proven to be effective when training. What is actually done during the break can vary. It could be repeating a well-established exercise, going for a short wander or allowing your horse to pick at some grass, in other words a brief moment for reflection and doing nothing. You can also take a break of a few days between individual units so that what has been learned has a chance to be fully digested and cemented into the horse's mind. Practising the same exercise daily does not guarantee faster progress.

When it's time to take a longer break

A horse doesn't automatically know when a training session starts and when it ends. For this reason it is important that, in addition to the horse being taught a sign that indicates when the end of a training session has been reached (see later), we also need to teach them a signal that indicates the start of a session. Such a signal will prove to be especially useful for your horse so that it knows when it should switch to a mood of high concentration and motivation from its normal relaxed mode. It is for this reason that schools ring a bell to mark when it is time for lessons or for breaks to begin. Children are thus given a sign that they need to start concentrating and another that they can let themselves go and have fun.

performance of certain behaviour, and the handler has to manage the process of delivering the rewards. Self-service on the horse's part is not allowed and will never lead to success. How the handler manages his supply of treats effectively is detailed from page 52.

The brain loves to take a break

Breaks are times during which the horse and, therefore, its handler are not having to concentrate on specific training goals. Positive training requires a high level of concentration from both participants, and so can be very demanding. Neither human nor horse can concentrate continuous-

How do you do this when training your horses? Every time you want to take a break from conditioning your horse with a target object, give a signal that indicates that you are going to take a

What has already been learned will be digested subconsciously during a break.

break, and put the target out of sight and reach of your horse. Such a signal might consist of the words "time out" or similar, but a hand signal or touching the horse's neck in a particular place or in a particular way will also do the job. You should then leave the horse and go to the edge of the school with as neutral an expression as possible and wait for the horse to drop its head or start to graze. Pay no attention to it and don't try to attract its attention back to you.

If you then want to continue training give a further signal, for example by saying the word "continue", retrieve the target and show it to the horse. At even the slightest indication by the horse towards the target or if it touches the object correctly click and reward to mark the continuation of the session, and with it the end of the break. At the end of the session you need to give your horse a further sign that work has ended and it can go back to its friends in the field to do what it wants. Use a further word such as "finished" or a specific pat on its back when you are putting it back out in the field, to mark the end of the period of concentration. After this point no further training should be done on that day.

In their free time horses should be allowed just to be horses.

a surprising win will create a clear boost in motivation and should create a lasting effect. The horse should remember with pleasure the behaviour that resulted in such a fantastic reward. However, awarding a jackpot is only sensible when there has been a particular breakthrough in training. Receiving, in effect, first prize shouldn't become a habit otherwise it will lose its appeal as well as its particular effect on the horse.

Do I always need to use feed as a reward?

Of course you don't always or exclusively have to reward with feed. Nevertheless, feed is a simple and practical form of reward that usually means

A jackpot might be a handful of the horse's favourite oats.

Hitting the jackpot

Just as in gambling, there are moments during the training of horses in which a large prize can be won. This so-called jackpot is a special form of reward that the horse only receives when it has really excelled and done something particularly well. The reward might be an especially coveted treat, a whole handful of oats or even a long scratch of a favourite spot.

Offering this jackpot prize in training is important both for the effect it has of being a total surprise and because the reward that is offered is a particularly desirable one for the horse. Such

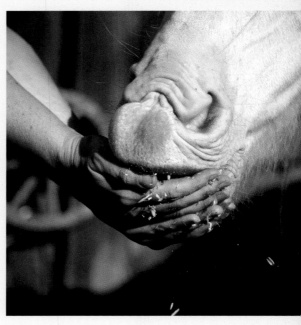

so much to a horse that it is prepared to perform demanding tasks for it. Few horses would be prepared to do a flying change for a quick pat on the neck. For a tasty treat of dried banana chips, though, things will look very different. The type of reward needs to be selected according to the individual tastes of each horse so that it is both enjoyable and something that the horse strives to receive. As well as edible treats many horses enjoy being scratched on the withers, neck or the top of the tail. They may also enjoy a quick game of tag, a warm and enthusiastic pat or even being given a toy to play with.

The objection to this method that you are stuffing your horse full or making it fat is easy to refute when you consider that for a typical training session you would only use about 200 grams (less than half a pound) of carrot pieces, of which the energy value is negligible.

Not every type of reward will prove to be practical for everyday use and in every situation. When riding you are not going to take along a large ball as a favourite toy to be offered as a reward, but instead you are more likely to use edible treats, a scratch or your own enthusiastic praise to win over your

Many horses love playing with a big ball.

Running together can be so much fun for many horses that it becomes self-rewarding behaviour.

ercises will become rewards in themselves. Many horses for example love the view they get when they are taught to climb up onto a step or small rostrum, and many also really seem to enjoy showing off in Spanish walk. Once learned, exercises such as these become a form of reward in themselves, becoming so-called self-rewarding behaviour.

Games to break the ice

The beginning of a new phase in the development of your communication with each other should be free of stress and filled with joy for both participants. This phase is not suited to solving specific problems, such as loading problems, or for training complex exercises, such as the different types of lateral movements. Instead you should try out learning games that you can play with your horses, during which the horse can get to know the rules of reward-based training and the handler learns the essential principles and the necessary timing, and gets a better idea of what they want to achieve.

Games in which the handler can control the beginning and the end of the exercise are best suited for this, such as games involving objects that can be removed easily from a horse's field of vision when the game is at an end.

Fetch the ball!

Show your horse a small soft ball and put it on the ground. Then train the horse to touch the ball with its mouth by clicking and rewarding every time it does it. When your horse can perform this action reliably go on to delay the click slightly. Your horse will get slightly irritated at this and will try to get you to click by experimenting

horse. You will really see the benefit once you realise that a reward can be anything that motivates a horse at that precise moment. A reward might be allowing a horse to graze along a path when it has just performed a task particularly well.

Imagine that your rewards are at different levels, with consolation prizes that are nice, second prizes that the horse enjoys and first prizes about which a horse can get really excited. The harder an exercise is and the more energy that has to be expended by the horse in doing it, the better the reward should be. As a result of a horse's enjoyment in learning, over a period of time certain ex-

with different types of additional behaviour. It may move the ball by tipping it with its nose or step on it with its hoof. You should wait until the horse happens to bite into the ball, clicking at exactly this point and providing it with the necessary tit-bit.

This now becomes the new criterion for giving a treat. You should from now on only offer a reward when the horse takes the ball into its mouth, repeating this sequence a number of times.

In order to start the actual fetching, don't put the object immediately in front of the horse, but throw it up to a metre away. You need to ensure that the distance isn't too great at first so that the horse is motivated to complete the task successfully. The horse should be rewarded for going to the ball and picking it up. Gradually increase the distance between the horse and the object .

Next you will need to work on the process of asking the horse to give you the ball. Do this by putting your hand underneath the horse's mouth when it is trying to hold the ball. At some stage the horse will let the ball go and it will fall into your hand. You should click at the exact moment when you catch the ball. Repeat this part of the exercise ten to fifteen times, until your horse understands the connection.

As the end result you want the horse to come towards you while carrying the object in its mouth. This means that you should gradually have less of a tendency to follow the horse towards the ball and instead wait for the horse to look for you and come towards you. The distance from where you are standing to where the horse picks up

Dinah has learned to fetch a ball.

the ball should be increased only very gradually because it is very difficult for a horse to hold something in its mouth for long periods of time. As with all exercises the appropriate muscles have to develop sufficient strength, and the horse's ability to concentrate must not be overtaxed.

It should take horse and handler several days to learn this exercise and its component parts. It is not the end result but the shared enjoyment in the many small learning successes that are the true purpose of this exercise.

In the next stage of training, Dinah learns to drop the ball into a bucket to receive a reward.

Thank you

Small children are usually praised effusively when they learn to tie their shoelaces. It makes the little ones proud, motivates them and encourages them to become more independent. The same procedure used with a teenager or even an adult would however seem very strange. The frequency and intensity of praise should always relate to the realistic ability of the person concerned. An adult would quite rightly feel silly if we reacted to some triviality by offering exaggerated praise. However, even as an adult it is satisfying when your partner thanks you now and then for something that is often taken for granted.

It is just the same with your horse; initially it should be thoroughly praised and rewarded for small successes. Gradually only the complicated exercises should be rewarded with constant praise. Don't forget, however, to say thank you every now and then for things that you would usually take for granted, because it is these small gestures that are the mark of a harmonious relationship. An animal needs to experience lots of small moments of pleasure and have the feeling of being valued and respected.

Training made fun –
professional tips and training tricks

Most riders don't know their horses from the day they are born and aren't responsible for the way they are raised. Instead they buy a horse that may have been trained up well or badly and that has a ready-formed personality with its own history. Just as the horse will have experienced certain things that we know nothing about, it will also probably have been confronted with a training method that involved a greater or lesser degree of force.

Training according to current traditional guidelines usually involves the principle of pressure and release, in other words working with varying degrees of pressure. A positive method of training seeks to create an atmosphere of learning that is free from the use of pressure and the threat of punishment. When beginning to change your methods you will encounter animals that have had a variety of previous experiences with their human training partners. In this cross-over period your horse has to learn that a whole different set of rules now apply. It is important however that the two different forms of training don't get mixed up with each other, and the handler must decide how to structure the time spent with their horse in the future. Working first using pressure and then with reward will in the longer term only serve to dilute both methods. If you were to offer a reward after carrying out an exercise that involves the use of pressure, after a while the pressure will be an indication that a reward will follow and this will make the pressure less and less effective. Use of this mixed method means that the horse will react less and less quickly. On the other hand, even a minimal use of pressure will weaken the value of a reward. The horse will become more and more insecure and in the future will cooperate less willingly and becomes less motivated in its work. Any change in the way a horse is trained must be obvious and be carried out systematically and consistently. In the transitional phase it will help for there to be a clear distinction made, perhaps by the horse wearing one headcollar for its standard work and a different one when doing clicker training.

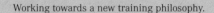

Working towards a new training philosophy.

What if your horse doesn't want to cooperate?

When a horse refuses to do something, the first question that should be asked is whether the horse is happy and healthy. Is it either physically or mentally ready to carry out what it is being asked to do, or is it being prevented from doing so by pain, trauma or illness? When you have excluded health-related issues as causes of reluctance or passivity, you should ask yourself why your horse should bother to follow your commands, and what you are offering them as an incentive. Motivation is the magic word when trying to gain cooperation and participation from your horse. Just as you do, a horse wants to be rewarded for its efforts. And, just as much, it also deserves the freedom of simply being allowed to be a horse without always being assessed on its performance.

Gloa has learned to turn her head politely away from the feed bowl so that she later gets a treat from the bowl.

The tit-bit monster

People who train horses using feed rewards are often accused of creating an unavoidable problem. The horse is supposed to suddenly mutate into an uncontrollable tit-bit monster, either begging for treats constantly or becoming a horse that bites. Initially this worry may seem justified because it really is very unpleasant if your horse becomes strongly fixated on the treats or tries to help itself. A horse that is constantly nudging you or trying to get into your pockets or treat bag is unpleasant, and can even become dangerous. Many horses that have previously been given treats only very occasionally, or those that are simply greedy, may to start with get very ex-

cited by this new way of training. Begging can even be selected for if you are imprecise in the way you give the horse its rewards, but this is not a result of training with feed rewards in general. In order to rid the equestrian world finally of this prejudice it needs to be stated clearly that begging, pushy behaviour or uncontrollable greed are the results of us giving our horses feed in a totally unstructured way. We have trained this undesirable behaviour into our horses, and by behaving incorrectly ourselves have reinforced it further. For this reason it is important that strict feeding rules be established for human participants, and appropriate politeness be expected from the equine participants, before training by reward is started.

A reward should only ever be offered away from the bag in which the treats are stored.

Feeding tips for training

Just as the reward sound tells the horse that it has earned a reward, it should also realise that no reward will be forthcoming if it doesn't hear the sound. This means that you should never give your horse a treat without first making the necessary noise. No exceptions to this rule should ever be made.

The use of a noise in connection with a reward only makes sense when the noise is made at exactly the same time as the desired behaviour, or the behaviour that we are trying to train, is exhibited. You have no more than two seconds in which to indicate to the horse that it has done the right thing. After this time, it won't connect the reward with what it has done and will no longer know what you were trying to reward.

This use of positive reinforcement is a very powerful tool, so you should always consider very carefully what it is that you want to reward. When your horse has done something, ask yourself whether it was really the behaviour that you want and a step on the way to your goal. If it wasn't, then giving a reward will create problems for you very quickly. Horses have no idea of what is right and what is wrong so they are just as quick to learn undesirable behaviour through rewards. Riders who complain about their horses begging usually only have themselves to blame, because they have effectively, albeit unintentionally, trained their horses to be like this. A horse should never be fed or rewarded when being rude or pushy.

Another important point is always to offer the reward on an outstretched hand and never directly next to your pocket because this will help to avoid encouraging the horse to try and root around in your pocket. For this reason, even if the horse is waiting for its treat with its mouth right next to your treat bag, you should always move your hand past its head and offer it to them away from you and the bag.

For reasons of safety, if you have a particularly pushy, greedy horse it is always a good idea to tie it up when starting this work, or position yourself behind a fence or stable door. This teaches the horse to control its greed without putting the handler in any danger.

Please, don't help yourself

A well-filled bag of treats is tempting for any horse. It is totally understandable that some horses will try to take the direct route to these treats. However, the point of reward-based training is not to allow the horse simply to help itself whenever it feels like it. The handler is responsible for distributing the treats from their supply only in return for a job performed, and they give the horse a positive

Any horse can learn to wait politely for the click and the treat if you follow the feeding rules carefully.

response by the use of the reward sound. The horse should understand the basic rule that it may never help itself. The horse won't know this automatically, so it has to learn gradually from you when it will receive a reward and when it won't.

A good way of making it clear to a horse how this system of rewards works is to start during the first exercises. Assume that you are just about to click when your horse is carrying an object. When offering the reward after the click make it clear that self-service is not an option by moving the treat, held in your closed hand, past the horse's waiting mouth and offering the treat to the horse well away from your body. Never give the horse a treat when it moves its head towards you or your bag.

Control signals – when the horse has learned its vocabulary

An impressive example of a control signal working: the horse lowers it head in response to a hand signal.

I often meet people who are experiencing the problem that their horse performs a task that they have trained it to do not just when it is asked for but whenever it wants to, or the horse uses it to beg for a treat. The reason for this is that the control signal is insufficient or lacking in some way. In general terms the signal that you give will be a stimulus that causes a certain behaviour or action to take place. The stimulus might be a sign made with your hand, a spoken command or even certain body language. You need to teach your horse the significance of this stimulus or sign during training with the use of lots of repetition and reward. You achieve total control over a certain exercise only when it is done specifically in response to the given cue and at no other time. In theory it is possible to control any behaviour totally using control signals. Practice has proven however that control signals are easily distracted from and are strongly influenced by whether a horse is motivated or not, so it is never really possible to control an animal's behaviour one hundred percent. A control signal does, however, help a horse to make the connection between a command given by the clicker and the reward

Bessi has learned to back up towards Verena when she gives a hand signal. Because of the success and enjoyment gained from this exercise Bessi will become increasingly sensitive to her handler's commands.

offered as a result of a successfully completed task.

An example of how control signals might be inadequate at first can be seen during the early stages of training a new exercise. You may wish, for example, to teach your horse through the use of rewards to do a Spanish walk. At the start of the lesson it is irrelevant whether you give a signal or not. The horse should always be rewarded when it offers any sign of a Spanish walk. Now comes the crucial part, in which the horse has to learn that its Spanish walk will only be rewarded when the signal is given. The signal could be pointing with your finger to its foreleg. Your horse

is likely to offer Spanish walk repeatedly, but it will learn through trial and error that it can only expect a reward when it performs the action after the hand signal has been given. Only then is the Spanish walk to any great extent controlled by a signal. You should try to ignore it when the horse offers you Spanish walk without being given a signal first. Not to do so could mean that in its enthusiasm the horse will tend to throw its forelegs about at any opportunity. If you are able to ignore this unwanted behaviour at this stage then it should soon stop.

If the handler is patient, a horse will soon learn that it is actually quite tiring to do Spanish walk constantly, especially when it is rewarded with neither attention nor a tit-bit, and that it is more worthwhile to wait for the appropriate signal to be given. How long it takes before a horse understands a specific signal will be dependent on the horse's temperament. In the case of especially demanding words in your shared vocabulary you should allow plenty of time for you both to learn them.

From clicker to clicking with your tongue

"I don't want to spend my entire life carrying a clicker around with me and constantly having to give my horse a treat for anything it does." This is one of the comments often made by people who have decided against a rewards-based system of training, until they are told that this is not necessarily the case. On the contrary, one of the goals of your later training is to establish a second reward sound that is very similar to the metallic click of the clicker. This new sound, clicking with your tongue, will be used in the future as a natural clicker. One of the big advantages of this is that you always have your tongue with you and won't be dependent on the clicker device. The other advantage is that you will have both hands free. If you would normally use a clicking sound as a signal for your horse to go faster, you should come up with a different sound, for example a kissing sound made with your lips. I still tend to train new exercises with the clicker, however, because the sound is clearer and

studies have shown that most people react more quickly with their hands than with their mouth.

Of course you will need to repeat each new exercise many times until it has been reasonably well understood, but you don't want to have to hand out a treat every few seconds for every small thing your horse

It's useful for your horse to learn to recognise the meaning of a tongue click.

does for the rest of your life. On the one hand you would never be able to achieve what you want to, and on the other hand it would very quickly become very boring for you and your horse. For this reason, for exercises in which your horse is reasonably well accomplished you should reduce the use of the clicker gradually and give rewards less and less frequently, and in return you should add new exercises to your repertoire to keep the horse motivated.

Be careful however that any reduction in the use of rewards (sound or tit-bits) is only introduced very gradually and that there is no pattern to the change. The horse should not be able to predict when it can expect a reward. A young horse, for example, should be rewarded every time it backs up correctly on command, while a more experienced animal should be rewarded less and less over time. If you work for too long using continuous reinforcement you will make your horse dependent on the presence of a reward. Your horse will become more fixated on being rewarded every time it does something. For this reason, as soon as the horse has understood the connection between your command for backing up and its resultant behaviour you should move on to a more variable and intermittent pattern of reward. That means that, depending on what you are aiming for and the horse's progress, you should offer a reward either every other time or only now and again (a fixed or variable reward rate). In addition you should be more flexible with regard to the length of time for which the horse is asked to perform the behaviour before it is offered a reward (fixed or variable length of behaviour). Within a training session the frequency of the reward should depend either on how often the desired behaviour is shown or on the length of time that it

is performed for. You should never work on both of these at the same time.

When it doesn't quite go to plan

For horses and their handlers that have been trained predominantly using conventional methods, problems can often occur when changing

By structuring your training cleverly you can avoid stressing your horse and reduce the likelihood of it becoming frustrated.

over to a more positive method of training because the rules of the game have also changed quite considerably. The following section runs through the most common types of problem and offers solutions.

Lacking patience

Many horses don't have a long concentration span and will try to do something or anything as quickly as possible just to earn reward. They won't try to find out what the actual task is that they are being asked to do. These horses are easily frustrated when their handler turns their attention back to the exercise without offering a tit-bit.

Over-motivated horses like these possess a very low frustration threshold. Even when positive training methods are used there is a risk of the horse becoming frustrated. As a consequence, stress levels will be raised uncomfortably, the horse will feel as if it is being overtaxed, and it will not be able to carry out the exercise in a relaxed or motivated manner.

In order to raise a horse's frustration threshold you will have to increase the difficulty of the exercise gradually, at the same time moving slowly from offering rewards constantly to more intermittently. Besides this gradual increase in the difficulty of a specific exercise it is also important to move from new exercises, with which the horse will quite quickly become frustrated, to older well-established tasks that it can succeed in very quickly. This to-and-fro will motivate your horse greatly and help it to get over any learning difficulties it may have with more demanding exercises.

At the same time however every horse should learn to endure a certain degree of frustration and control its emotions. A good opportunity to practise this occurs when feeding a horse that is tied up. Any horse will want to get to the feed as quickly as possible by trying to get to its feed bucket. As soon as you see the horse doing this stop straight away and don't go any closer to the horse. Even if it starts to paw the ground or move around you need to stay still or move away with the bucket. As soon as it stops pawing or moves back even slightly, then it should be given its feed immediately. The horse learns from this how to control its unacceptable behaviour and to accept you as the person who controls access to its feed.

Being a jack of all trades

Particularly when working with feed as a reward, you will come across horses that are so thrilled by their work with you that they don't know what to do with all that stored-up energy. Without being asked, they will perform their entire repertoire of tricks in the vague hope that the behaviour you are looking for will crop up at some stage. With hotheads like this you must pay particular attention to creating a link between a control signal and an action from the start. You should never work on the exercise that the horse happens to perform or present to you first. Ignore this one-horse show and give the already established signal for the movement that you want to work on. This signal could be a hand sign, a verbal command or body language, and will depend again on the exercise to be performed and the level of

A motivated and spirited horse is something truly wonderful – as long as you can direct all that pent-up energy.

training. In the case of over-motivated horses you should also move between faster, active tasks and slower, calmer tasks. Horses should never feel that training means getting over-excited and having the opportunity to do what they want. Changing the type of reward from feed treats to physical contact such as patting or scratching can also be a way to get a horse's attention and to calm it down. In the case of a very hyperactive horse the line

between enjoyment and overdoing it is a very fine one.

Poisoned cues

If a horse is difficult to encourage to do even the easiest of exercises, despite having an engaged and motivated handler and plenty of rewards being offered then it is likely to be suffering from a lack of motivation. You will have to tackle the phenomenon of "poisoned cues". Every living creature has its own history and may have had an experience in its past that has given something that you are doing quite innocently a negative connotation. Something that may appear to be totally innocuous could be for your horse a trigger for something unpleasant being about to happen. This might be either a wrongly used signal, a command that had been trained using pressure or a punishment of some kind, or even an event that happens to be associated with some type of behaviour. Poisoned cues can consist of anything from smells or noises to touches or common objects – anything that a horse connects with something unpleasant happening.

Let's assume that your horse hates having its saddle put on. At some stage it was perhaps ridden with a poorly fitting saddle and as a result connects the sight of a saddle with having a sore back. To solve the problem you will no doubt call in a saddle fitter to fit a saddle properly and try to change the horse's attitude towards its saddle. This will only be successful if you take into consideration all the signals that "poisoned" the action of putting the saddle on the horse. In one case that I am aware of the poisoned cue was the metallic clinking of the girth buckles in the tack room. The horse had associated this noise negatively with the chain of events that ran "noise – saddling – mounting – pain". If you want to solve a problem like this you have first of all to identify the poisoned cue and then find the antidote. The noise that has this negative connotation must no longer be an advance warning of pain but instead you have to turn it into a sign that something enjoyable is about to happen. You shouldn't even start with the saddle, but should establish a positive link with the sound of the girth by offering a treat every time the horse hears the girth clinking until its negative behaviour or any other sign of stress is no longer shown.

Discovering these poisoned signals, which may be often well hidden, requires a nose for detection and a lot of patience, but you should be prepared to take up the challenge if you want to have a relationship with your horse that is not predicated on fear. In the case of some problem horses there may unfortunately be a whole chain of poisoned cues that can only be found one after the other. In addition to recognising the individual signal that has been infected you need to define it anew and give it a positive connotation. You may also decide to introduce totally new signals. A horse that sees the bit as a poisoned cue may be able to be ridden again in a bitless bridle because this type of bridle doesn't have a negative connotation.

To avoid even the risk of creating a poisoned cue it is sensible to tackle putting the bridle on for the first time in as small steps as possible. Click and reward every positive action made by the horse, such as putting its head into the bridle, until it could almost put it on itself.

The trick with the stick –
target training

Depending on what you are trying to achieve and the situation you are working in, there are a variety of aids and methods that belong to the toolkit of any positive horse trainer. Target training plays a very important role in the education of your horse. Using this process your horse learns the meaning of different objects and being touched with them on different parts of its body. It will learn to follow a stick or a hand signal, to stand on or next to a marker, or to move towards it. These target objects help a horse to assess a situation accurately and enable us to begin new exercises without having to put the horse under any pressure. The targets become easily identifiable signs that also show the horse what behaviour or action is required. Targets are an indispensable tool for positive training.

The diversity of target training

Depending on the individual exercise, targets can take the form of a wide variety of objects. The most well known are long sticks, known as "target sticks", that a horse is sup-

Naeryo follows the new target as if there were an invisible lead rope connecting the two.

posed to follow and that can also be used as an aid to lead the horse. Long objects such as telescopic poles are particularly well suited for this, although fly swats, kitchen spoons, bamboo sticks or whips are suitable, providing the latter don't have any negative associations for the horse. It is particularly important that the part of the stick that the horse is going to be asked to touch, usually the tip, is easily identifiable to the horse and can be distinguished by the horse from the rest of the stick. In the case of fly swats this is obvious. With bamboo sticks you can wrap the end of the stick with coloured insulation tape or stick a tennis ball on the end. Having a target stick with a rounded end or one with a ball on the end means not only that the tip is easily identifiable, but also that you can't hurt the horse by accidentally prodding it in the nose.

The first time the horse encounters the target stick an initial process of operant conditioning occurs. As already detailed on page 26 you should hold the stick next to the horse's mouth so that it touches it, either by accident or out of curiosity. You should mark this immediately with the reward sound and a treat. Given that the horse has already been conditioned to the click it should understand after only a few repetitions that the stick is what you want it to touch with its nose or mouth.

In the next stage of training the horse needs to learn to follow the target and to touch it regardless of where it goes. You should begin to move the stick around into different positions, first higher and then lower, and then between the horse's

Target training is a very motivating type of work. Some horses just can't get enough of it and will ask you to continue the game by bringing a target to you.

forelegs so that the horse has to look for the target actively in order to touch it and earn its click and then its reward. You should only extend the distance of the object from the horse's nose bit by bit so that the horse doesn't lose interest in following the target. Gradually it should be asked to stretch to touch the target further away.

Once it can do this, you can begin to position the target far enough away to require the horse to take a step to be able to touch it. It will need to walk towards the object and then touch it in order to get its click and reward. In the next stage you can help to cement what has been learned by walking slowly ahead of the horse with the stick in your hand. Only offer the reward when your horse follows you at the required tempo, almost as if you are holding a giant magnet in your hand.

With a little practice your horse can learn to follow the target over longer distances at a variety of paces and speeds. You will be able to lead your horse without any direct attachment between you and the horse, as if you have an invisible lead rope, and you can then try more difficult variations such as leading your horse through a maze of poles or slalom down a line of cones. You will also soon be able to call your horse to come to the target and use this, for example, to call it in from the field over greater distances.

Morghain has learned to lock on
to Ursula's hand and follow
this hand-target. The two are
now ready to start more
advanced liberty work.

Follow me – practical hand-target training

Building on the work done with the target stick, the horse can now learn to follow the handler freely, with the help only of the invisible lead rope. In the case of this hand-target training the teacher's hand becomes the target for the horse to touch. Our long-term goal is to be able to lead our horse without using a halter or lead rope or any other aids. It will also help us later to be able to direct the horse's nose into the required position when we are working on circus tricks or gymnastic types of exercise.

First you have to decide on a specific signal to be given with your hand when you are using it as a hand-target. It needs to be unmistakable for the horse, so could be a clenched fist or a pointed finger with an outstretched arm. If the horse is holding its nose at the same level as your hand click and offer a reward. After several repetitions, and just as you changed the position of your hand when training with the stick, switch from the left to the right hand and again reward the horse for following it with its nose. Once the horse starts to move actively towards your hand you can begin to walk the first few steps with them. At the start of this exercise only ask for a very few steps before you click and give a treat so that the horse continues to enjoy its work. Later the horse should only be rewarded when it has walked a longer distance with you with its head level with your hand. You should always vary the direction and the speed to make the exercise more interesting.

When you have reached a stage where your horse follows you with ease you can start to integrate target training into your daily routine and combine it with other exercises. Your horse should now follow your hand voluntarily in the hope of being rewarded and so can adapt its speed to your own without you needing a whip or pulling it along with the lead rope. You should of course only practise loose leading in a well-fenced area for reasons of safety.

The whip as a target

Whips can also be used as targets because they can help to give the horse a visual aid to indicate the direction in which you are asking it to move

Alex uses her whip to show Selena which foreleg she should raise at this stage of her Spanish walk.

a specific part of its body. In positive training the whip is never used as something for the horse to move away from but quite the opposite. A whip used in a positive sense actually acts as a magnet, pulling the horse towards it. In line with the method described above for the target stick, the horse should first be rewarded with a click and a treat every time it moves its leg towards the whip positioned next to it. In doing this it learns to match the level of its foreleg to that of the whip. An example of how this can be used is in teaching the Spanish walk. After your horse has learned to lift the appropriate leg when touched with the whip, you can refine the degree to which it lifts and stretches its leg by indicating with the target object - your whip - the height that you require the leg to be lifted to. The expression in your horse's Spanish walk can thus be improved more easily and you are in a position to be able to communicate precisely the level of improvement required.

Stationary targets – places of safety

As well as using moveable targets, which are ideal when asking the horse to follow you or to get the horse to move in a specific pattern, you can also work with fixed or static targets, in other words targets that stay in one place and don't move towards or around the horse. Static targets should be touched until either a new command is issued to change the horse's behaviour or a click is used to signal the end of the exercise. A variety

of objects can be tried such as mats, lids or poles laid out on the ground. A small pedestal or block can be used as a static target if it gives the horse enough space to stand up on with its forelegs. Static targets are easily recognised by horses and create a sense of security and calm when trying new exercises or when working in unfamiliar surroundings.

Horses are very inventive when it comes to attracting our attention by doing something that we don't want them to do! You can counter this problem by establishing another type of behaviour because it will be difficult for a horse to exhibit undesirable behaviour at the same time as it is being asked to do something completely different. If a horse paws the ground when tied up for grooming you can use a fixed target to distract it. Teach it to touch the target quietly and thus convert the pawing into more desirable behaviour. The target might be a plastic lid attached to the ring that the horse is tied up to, or a rubber mat on the floor that the horse is asked to touch while it is being brushed. You should teach the horse to touch the target first and then, depending on the attention span of the horse, extend the length of time for which the horse is required to stand calmly next to it or stand on it. The length of time for which you ask your horse to do nothing should only be increased gradually, with plenty of short breaks in between, so that it doesn't get frustrated and lose interest.

The touch signal

After the initial stages of working with a target, just catching a glimpse of an object will cause a horse to react with the behaviour associated

Gloa waits patiently on the mat for Verena's signal.

with it. When it sees the visual signal, in other words the target stick, your horse will want to touch it. In order to be able to utilise this with more flexibility in different situations, it will prove useful to introduce a vocal signal that indicates when you want the horse to touch the object. Your horse should now learn to touch the target when given the vocal command. Many trainers use the word "touch".

Start introducing this new word by saying it just before you show the horse the target. Later, during the exercise only reward the horse for touching the target when you have given the command. With time the horse will associate the word "touch" with touching objects in general. In doing this your horse is actually showing an astonishing ability for abstract thinking, similar to our own, in being able to understand a word used in different contexts. In other words it is able to understand and interpret the same command used for a variety of different objects.

The intellectual ability necessary to do this will also prove to be extremely useful

Bessi recognises the signal to touch given by Verena and bends around to reach her clenched fist. This makes a game out of suppling exercises.

when introducing new targets later in every-day training. You can use this to make new or spooky objects more palatable. You "sell" them simply as new targets, using the command to touch them to ask your horse to make contact with them. Using this method, most horses very quickly get used to a huge range of objects such as scary tarpaulins, rubbish bins or plastic tape.

A shower of treats

A heavy rubber mat such as those used in stables or trailers can become an important aid when training your horse. Train your horse to touch it with all four feet by teaching it to stand on it and stay there quietly. Praise and reward the horse every time it touches the mat with a hoof, and then later just for standing quietly on the mat.

Use of the so-called shower of treats can be very motivating in a number of exercises where the horse is being asked to stay in one position. As soon as the horse is standing quietly on the mat imagine that you are turning on a shower that pours treats out, rather than water. Click and reward every second that it remains still and in contact with the static target. As soon as the horse moves even one hoof, stop immediately as if you have turned off the tap. This sharp contrast helps the horse understand that standing quietly is by far the more rewarding option. As training progresses you should reduce the frequency and amount of treats offered to a more manageable level. Using this technique the mat itself becomes a positively reinforced location and in itself is a form of reward.

You can now include this in your selection of exercises by, for example, doing a figure of eight,

When your horse has reached an important milestone it should be showered with treats.

crossing over the mat positioned in the centre of the eight and using it as a target and reward point. You can also use it as a motivating factor to encourage your horse to load onto a trailer when it is resistant, or allow the horse to take a rest by standing on the mat after working on something it finds hard such as shoulder-in.

It's not reaching the destination but the journey that counts –
shaping behaviour

One of the most interesting training concepts is shaping. No horse is going to start doing Spanish walk spontaneously in the hope that we will notice and start to praise it. Horses have no idea what we are aiming for when we start training and are very unlikely to show a perfect end result by chance. Shaping behaviour means working towards your goal step by step, accompanying your horse along the way with clicks and rewards.

To help you, imagine your horse doing a perfect Spanish walk in slow motion and observe which muscle is being used when. It is vitally important that you form an exact picture of what you are trying to achieve for each exercise, behaviour or movement. Now you need to turn this picture, for example of a perfect Spanish walk, into reality by breaking it down into miniscule steps and marking and rewarding even the smallest of muscle twitches from the muscle groups involved in the movement, rather than just the end result. This is what we call micro-shaping.

You don't even need to touch your horse, but use rewards to guide your horse's behaviour in the direction of what you are trying to achieve, moving from attempt to attempt and gradually getting closer to the end result.

This process is similar to the games children play at parties when one is blindfolded and is guided in the direction of the prize by the others shouting "hot" or "cold". This is a classic example of shaping. Only the surrounding players know where the finishing point is and the blindfolded player is totally reliant on the verbal clues. Despite not being able to see they will still reach their prize eventually.

However, if the child, or your horse, is told "you're going the wrong way" or "that's not right" too often during the shaping process they will become discouraged and they will quickly be demotivated. The result is that their reactions will become increasingly passive, or they will become so frustrated that they won't want to "play" anymore. To prevent your horse reaching this stage of helplessness only use positive signals during shaping to show what is right and ignore the mistakes that will inevitably happen during any process of learning.

Shaping is an extremely motivating learning concept that can be used in all areas of training. It is however, for both the handler and the horse, a very demanding way of learning and requires that you watch carefully for the subtlest of alterations in your horse's body language and the smallest signs of progress.

Basic shaping – the hula hoop game

A hula hoop bought from your local toy store can be used to show a classical example of how shaping can be used to train a trick. Put the hoop on the ground in front of your horse and mark each time your horse touches it with its muzzle. Refine your criteria millimetre by millimetre, only clicking and rewarding when the horse's top lip touches the upper part of the ring and the lower lip the lower side of the ring – in other words the preliminary step to actually biting onto it. Wait to click next when your horse opens its mouth and lightly bites the ring. From now on you should only click and reward the horse for holding the ring, even briefly, in its mouth. Next mark and reward the attempt to lift the ring up when the horse lifts its head. Initially, your horse will probably only lift the ring up briefly, before gradually trying to get the ring into a better position to throw it. As the exercise progresses, your horse will develop a better throwing technique until it manages to throw the hoop over its head by chance. At this stage you should give exaggerated praise with a well-earned jackpot.

The path to learning

To use shaping most effectively to change or create a specific type of behaviour you

Dinah is a hula hoop professional. Using shaping she has been taught to throw the hoop up and catch it over her head.

need to study how learning actually takes place and the route that it follows. In the long term you will want your horse to display a certain behaviour or action in the right place at the right time and in a certain context. By using body language or structuring the development of the lesson skilfully you can help the shaping process move in a specific direction from the start, so that mistakes are less likely to happen. You can help your horse to succeed faster just by conducting your training in surroundings that support the process, or through your own body language. For example, when starting to teach a horse to back-up, position your horse next to a fence or the edge of your arena, or use your own position next to the horse to prevent its quarters from swinging out.

Prompting: showing the way

A prompt is a teaching aid, an additional pointer or signal that either helps the horse to understand what you are trying to teach or indicates to it where the learning process is heading. Your own behaviour can be a prompt if, for example, you indicate by use of your own body language in which direction you want the horse to move, or start to run to cause your horse to change its pace. These special kinds of prompt are known as response-prompts.

You are using response-prompts as learning aids in the shaping process when you:

- give familiar verbal aids, such as raising the tone of your voice to urge the horse forward or dropping the tone to calm and encourage

- use gestures, imitation or body language as signals, such as making yourself smaller so as not to upset a timid horse or focusing your gaze on a specific part of the horse's body

- show your horse how to do something to encourage it to imitate and follow you, such as jumping over cavaletti in front of your horse.

In addition the entire surroundings and the atmosphere for learning that you create can serve as pointers. Reference points such as these are known as environmental prompts. You need to design your training environment in such a way as to increase the likelihood of the desired behaviour being learned successfully. The role of environmental prompts can be seen even more clearly in the use of a halter and lead rope to restrict the horse's movement and thus direct its behaviour along the desired track. Placing poles to create alleys or using cones as optical markers can be helpful environmental prompts when starting to loose school.

Fading – reducing the volume

You will of course also want to reduce the number of signs that you need to give your horse as training progresses. At some stage during shaping your horse should learn to respond to one definitive, single command to show a required action rather than needing a series of them. In a riding context a horse shouldn't just fall into canter because it is following behind a more experienced horse and responding to your voice as a response prompt, but be able to respond just to your physical aid. This method of reducing prompts is described in positive horse training as the process of "fading".

Fading is a process that transfers control from one or more stimuli to a signal or command chosen

Here Verena steps sideways, crossing one leg over the other in a response-prompt to help shape Bessi's lateral movements.

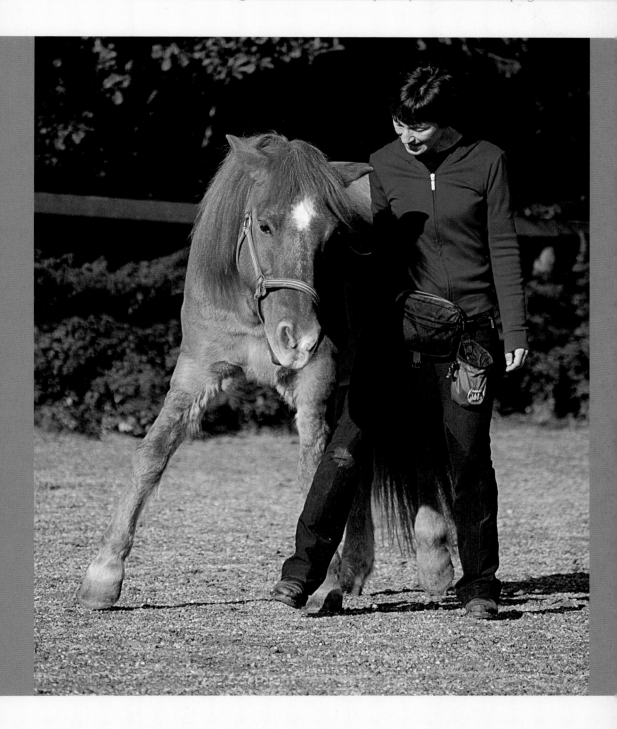

later. Your prompts fade increasingly to make way for what will become a set command. Using the example of loose schooling, after a period during which the horse trots around between parallel poles set out in a circle, the poles are removed one by one until you do away with the optical aids completely and your horse can move around you on a circle without a lunge rope.

When leading you can gradually put the lead rope over the horse's neck for longer periods until you can do away with it completely.

You can reduce your own physical response-prompts by selecting only one of the range of aids that you have been using (gesture, body position or voice) to become the single hand sign or voice command. Do this by gradually reducing the frequency with which you use the other prompts and put increased emphasis on the one signal that you have chosen to use in the future to ask for the required action or behaviour.

Tips on Fading:

1. Before you can even begin fading you need to decide what exactly you want the horse to do (i.e. its behaviour or action) and the exact signal that you are going to use to ask for it. For example, you want the horse to canter on the lunge from a single command without retaining the other aids you have used in teaching it to do this.

2. First you need to identify clearly all of the other prompts you have been using and be clear about their order so that they can be reduced accordingly. In the case of our cantering example you will probably have used both physical prompts, such as standing up straighter or running with the horse, and your voice, giving commands learned during other in-hand work, as well as environmental prompts, such as always asking the horse to canter in the same place on the circle.

3. You need to recognise the key stimuli, in other words the most important signals, and only slowly reduce

these so as to avoid any misunderstandings. You must ask yourself the question whether or not a specific and particularly effective prompt might later be used as the single definitive command, which will make the fading process much easier. As a rule, horses tend to react more strongly to aids given through body language, so it is often easier and more effective to use a physical prompt as your final command rather that insisting on a voice command. This poses the question, when you are lungeing, whether the horse sees the little hop on the spot you give, as if you were starting to canter, as a greater stimulus and finds it more important than the voice command given at the same time which it hardly pays any attention to. In this case you would need to reduce the prompt given by your body language only very slowly, or possibly use it as the main command and stop using the voice command totally.

4. If something starts to go wrong you will have to go back a step and use the key stimuli and stronger prompts you used before. Should your horse not respond to your command to canter, re-introduce the faded prompts in reverse order again.

The imaginary window of opportunity

By setting yourself an imaginary window of opportunity it is possible to speed up your horse's reaction to a signal or command that has already

By using an imaginary time frame you will increase the speed of your horse's reaction and reduce any time wasted in training. Thanks to Kerstin's motivating support, Jimmy is working with her enthusiastically.

been learned. For this purpose give your horse a well-established signal, such as "come". Imagine a specific time frame within which the signal has to be followed, for example five seconds. If the horse reacts within the given time it should be rewarded with a click and a treat. If it reacts too slowly there is no reward. In the course of a lesson, shorten the time frame until your horse only gets a reward if it responds immediately and without hesitation. Your horse's attention will be heightened and it will react much quicker, meaning less time will be wasted when training.

If you decide to use this concept it can be very helpful to imagine the signal to be like a set of traffic lights. When training a specific task you are working when the light is amber, meaning "Pay attention, something is about to happen and you have to react". The "internal" light then changes to green, opening a window of time, just as it does for a driver, within which we have to be able to react. You may develop this window of time either within the exercise or you can signal to the animal that a time frame exists by saying "quickly" to encourage it to hurry up. If your horse responds within the time allocated it should be rewarded, if not the light automatically turns red. It is then too late for a reward and the horse will have to wait for another opportunity to react faster, which when training should of course be provided as quickly as possible.

This method will prove to be particularly useful for exercises in which the horse has to learn to respond faster but without the use of pressure, for example going from working to medium trot. It can even help for you to encourage your horse on, almost like a cheerleader, to make it really clear that you want an increased tempo.

The starter – a momentary burst of enthusiasm

A starter is a taste of the rewards to follow. At the start of training or before a specific exercise some of the treats are revealed, and some are also given to the horse after a click, without it actually having had to do anything for them. This serves, as it were, as something to whet the horse's appetite and give it a burst of enthusiasm. The horse will now want to work in order to get further rewards.

This is also one of the reasons why many of us like gambling. The organiser offers a jackpot that we want to win, so we are prepared to pay to have a chance of winning it. If we didn't know what was in the jackpot we would be less likely to want to take part.

Starters are used in positive training especially when, for example, you are taking part in a show or a test. By giving your horse a few clicks and a few treats beforehand you start out with a much more motivated horse. Starters are also used to sweeten up a horse to an exercise that either it may not like or it finds difficult to do. In the case of such tasks as loading you will know beforehand whether a horse is going to be terribly enthusiastic or not. Quiet or sensitive horses that are of the passive but stressed

A small sample can sweeten the start when training more demanding exercises

type tend to be less willing to move and will barely trust themselves to try to do anything independently. You are faced with the problem that you can only offer very few rewards because the horse will rarely follow your instructions. The result is a very low rate of reward, which will in turn demotivate the horse further.

The starter gives you the opportunity to raise some enthusiasm for the work to come and give the horse a feeling of success before you even start training. Your horse will remain motivated and will make faster progress in its training. In addition the shyer equine personality is brought out of its shell because it quickly notices that the task is worth doing and it doesn't have to worry about being put under any pressure.

The starter should always be a particularly desirable reward that suits the individual taste of each horse. The horse should not be led through the exercise with a starter; the starter is only given before the exercise. Of course if the horse does the exercise successfully the rest of the starter can be used as a reward. Not to do so would cause your horse to be disappointed because you held the promise of this reward out at the start of the lesson and it will be looking forward to receiving more.

Creating happiness

Horses that have been trained using shaping gradually also start to learn independently. They tend to be very alert, focused and interested in the work they are doing with their handlers. They will also be able to express their own creativity if you allow them to. What may seem to be rather pointless games incorporating objects are especially suited to this purpose. The horse will develop its own variations and its handler can play along without caring about whether this kind of play could ever be turned into a trick to be performed on command. At the same time the ability of the horse to think for itself will be greatly increased.

In the course of time a horse will start to pick up more quickly on what its handler wants. It will become more involved in the training and it will sort itself out much faster in new situations or when faced with new or different objects, because it will no longer perceive something new as a threat, but rather as a challenge. A horse that is already familiar with a ball will not find a tarpaulin on the ground to be anything particularly special if you introduce it to them as a game as well.

As you have already seen, shaping is an extremely effective method of training. The horse learns quickly and retains what it has learned. There is another reason why I would also recommend this way of moulding a horse's behaviour. Shaping makes horses and their handlers and owners happy. When rewards are given the reward centre in the brain is activated in both human and horse, resulting in feelings of happiness. A horse obviously feels good when being trained in this way because it can determine the speed at which it learns and there are no restrictions that could cause stress or worry.

Capturing – seizing the moment

A method that is widely used in positive horse training when teaching certain patterns of behaviour is called capturing. Certain types of behaviour are now and again

Shaping simply makes you happy.

In positive horse training you often work with a horse's natural behaviour, for example rolling, and use clicking and rewards to teach the horse to lie down on command.

exhibited voluntarily, allowing them to be marked by a click and then rewarded. After several repetitions the horse will become aware that the specific behaviour shown has now become an exercise. One example of an easy to follow capturing exercise is to teach a horse to lie down. When you notice that your horse is about to lie down to roll mark this action immediately with a click. After only a few repetitions the horse will lie down deliberately while keeping its gaze on you and will make the connection

with receiving a treat. You can now introduce a sign such as a pointed finger and always use this when the horse lies down of its own volition, and later when you want it to lie down on command. You have thus captured this specific and natural movement successfully and can then recreate it. The advantages of capturing are that the tasks are easy for the horse to do and that the sequence of actions follows the animal's own natural movement. Teaching a horse to lie down in the classical way by asking it to bow and then kneel down has the advantage that it follows a set sequence of individual steps, but the action can appear artificial and very studied.

The support signal – giving a sense of security

Imagine that, rather than having been shaped, your horse can already master a certain task and there is no need to refine the exercise further or try something new. You would just like to indicate that the level that has now been reached should be maintained. Your horse should no longer be in training mode with its attention fo-cused, but should be in a more relaxed state. In addition to the "keep going" signal that I will explain later, you can also introduce another signal that tells your horse that an exercise has reached its conclusion and that no further improvements will be expected of it. This support signal means, in effect, "stay" and tells the horse that the exercise won't be modified and that they don't need to do anything further. You aren't trying, as you are with the clicker, to mark a specific event or action, but instead you need to use a more long drawn out tone like "gooooooooood" or "schhhhhhhhhhhh" to accompany the horse when it is performing the exercise in the way you wish.

Conny's support signal shows her horse Dinah that nothing more is expected of her than standing quietly.

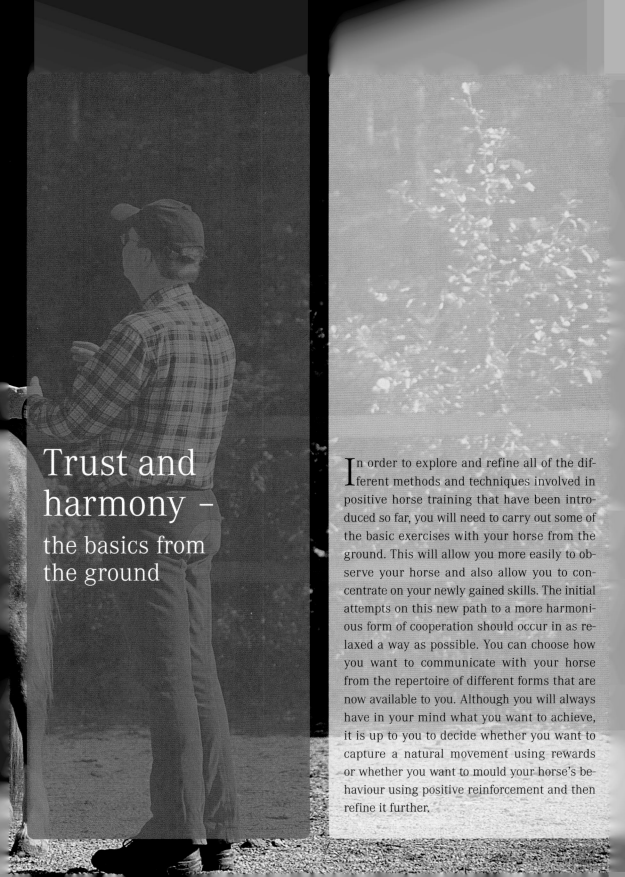

Trust and harmony –

the basics from the ground

In order to explore and refine all of the different methods and techniques involved in positive horse training that have been introduced so far, you will need to carry out some of the basic exercises with your horse from the ground. This will allow you more easily to observe your horse and also allow you to concentrate on your newly gained skills. The initial attempts on this new path to a more harmonious form of cooperation should occur in as relaxed a way as possible. You can choose how you want to communicate with your horse from the repertoire of different forms that are now available to you. Although you will always have in your mind what you want to achieve, it is up to you to decide whether you want to capture a natural movement using rewards or whether you want to mould your horse's behaviour using positive reinforcement and then refine it further.

By putting trust in your horse you are creating a firm emotional foundation for your future relationship that will help to reinforce the quality of your work together. The first lessons should be fun for the horse and handler team, stimulating creativity and making you curious as to how you can expand your communication and better recognise and respond to your horse's body language. With patience and empathy you will soon experience many moments of satisfaction and enjoyment on the path towards your goals, when you see understanding dawn in your horse's eyes and it surprises you with its sharp intelligence.

Standing still – the statue

If you want to teach your horse to stand still on command without being tied up (in Western riding circles this is called ground tying) there are a number of different methods. You can either encourage your horse to keep all four legs still and use a mat as an environmental prompt, or you can use response-prompts to form the appropriate behaviour. Do this by leading your horse beside you and then stop suddenly. Most horses will instinctively follow the movement of their handler and will also stand still. Mark the moment precisely at which all four legs come to a halt and praise the horse exaggeratedly.

When the horse responds consistently to your body's stop sign, introduce a voice command which in the future will be used to ask for the halt, such as "stop". Once the association between the body and vocal signal is securely established, delay your click so you build up more and more time, because you want the horse to stand still for longer periods and not just for a few seconds. If your horse moves before you click you have probably waited too long. In this case stop the exercise and try it again later.

You can then begin to increase the degree of difficulty. Give the command to "stop" and step back a few steps or walk in a circle around your horse, make sounds or wave an object about. Click at irregular intervals as long as the horse doesn't react and stays in place. After every click, make sure that you go up to the horse and give it a tit-bit and then continue with the exercise. This increase in difficulty should only be demanded gradually. The statue exercise is one of the basic exercises and is an essential skill for medical training, which we will describe later, as well as for versatility training.

Training for safety

We take horses out of their natural environment and put them into our modern and technology-filled world as companions and pets. They are subjected to a variety of outside stimuli such as traffic and colourful objects, and are also faced with the necessity of having medical treatment. Mother Nature hasn't equipped them for dealing with all of these challenges and influences. A relationship based on trust and the use of

Skadi masters the statue exercise under difficult circumstances and can even manage to swing a ball.

Using a syringe filled with apple sauce will make worming a lot more palatable later.

positive reinforcement can help your horse to deal with the demands of everyday life.

Zoos around the world have shown that trust can be created to a high level, even with wild animals, by using positive reinforcement to establish channels of communication. Flamingos can be led to a pond with the help of a target stick, elephants can enjoy a pedicure on a footstool, and rhinos will press up against the bars of their cage so that blood samples can be taken. A giant killer whale will show its trainer its impressive set of teeth to make the vet's job easier.

Besides the trust they have in their human trainers, all this is only made possible without the aid of tranquillisers by training the animals systematically. The knowledge gained by those who work with captive animals benefits you and your horse because you can learn from their methods of training, which were developed primarily to allow medical treatment, how to teach your horse to stand quiet and relaxed while having a poultice applied to its foot or while it is having its temperature taken, without the need of a twitch or sedation.

Over a number of training sessions and in small steps you can imitate and practise certain typical routine examinations. If you want to be able to open your horse's mouth

Imitating a visiting vet with accompanying clicks and rewards is a good dry run for the dreaded vaccination.

without using force, so that the vet can later check its teeth, start to accompany every brief touch of the mouth with a click. Pay attention that the horse keeps its mouth still and doesn't try to investigate your fingers or pull its head back. Gradually get closer to its lips until you can pull them apart gently. Continue to click and reward any new touches to the mouth to help make the unusual contact as acceptable as possible. The point of this training is to have the horse allow you to examine its teeth and gums without resistance. Parallel to this you can work in a similar way on lifting its tail and inserting a thermometer, bandaging its legs or listening to its heart, by using rewards and always waiting for moments of calm that can be rewarded. Fill a syringe with apple sauce to prepare your horse for being wormed. With all these exercises it is important that the horse is given the time it needs and that you don't make the mistake of wanting to do it all too quickly.

Besides becoming familiar with different types of routine treatment this training principle can be used to familiarise horses with unfamiliar objects they are likely to encounter when out and about, such as plastic bags, loud tractors or exploding balloons. Just as with target training (refer to pages 63–71), the horse can discover common objects at its own pace and learn to face the big wide world. There are no limits to your imagination when it comes to getting a horse used to the outside world.

Lower your head!
Relaxation for body and soul

Any horse can learn to lower its head on a given signal, to round its back, drop its neck and relax into a stretched outline, without the need of gadgets or other means of force. By lowering its head your horse assumes a more relaxed outline, which also has a positive effect on its behaviour.

You can wait for a moment when your horse happens to drop its head, such as when it sees something interesting on the floor and lowers its head to investigate. At this point you capture the action with a click and a reward, repeating this to establish an appropriate control signal.

Alternatively, try to entice the horse to lower its head with a treat. If your horse holds its head in the position that you want

It's good to practise tubbing a hoof and make it a positive experience before it is really necessary.

give it a positive sign with the click and a treat to follow. Gradually move on to holding your hand underneath the horse's head to encourage it down, linking this with a signal such as the word "down". You can move on gradually to giving a reward only when the horse keeps it head down for a given time, and then slowly extend this time.

Once your horse responds to the voice command when standing still, you can move on to asking it to lower its head at the walk. Put the horse on the lunge or lead it in hand and give your command. If the horse gives the slightest sign of a response, mark and reward even the smallest lowering of its head with a treat. Then you can once again carefully start to reward the horse when it keeps this lowered position for a certain time. You can also vary your demands in terms of the level the head is held at, millimetre by millimetre, until the horse is holding its head at the desired height. As your horse exhibits this behaviour more consistently over time you can also use this method of communicating what you want in the trot and canter. With horses that find it difficult to transfer this exercise from standing into movement you may find it useful to use a pole lying on the ground to help. It serves as an environmental prompt as well as an optical aid. When you ask your horse to approach the pole it will lower its head to look at the pole more clearly. Use this moment to click and offer a reward and then later practise without the pole.

One of the most significant advantages of learning by reward can be seen when lungeing your horse because you can give positive feedback on correct behaviour at exactly the right time and from a distance. When lungeing you are standing relatively far away from your horse and normally couldn't give it a reward at the precise moment it

The outstretched flattened hand held over the withers is a clear signal for the horse to lower its head.

lowers its head into the position you desire. If you are using a sound to reward the horse you can work on its outline, because during conditioning it has learnt that the click is used in conjunction with another reward such as feed. When it hears the click it will usually stop what it is doing to stand still and wait to be given its treat. Given that horses always tend to show the behaviour

Marking the exact moment when the horse drops and stretches its head and neck will encourage a good outline on the lunge.

that has in the past been most worthwhile, in the future it will start to hold its head in the lowered position more often and without being asked to do so. In addition your horse will show more enthusiasm for its work on the lunge because the rewards offered occasionally during the work will act to motivate it even more and make the process even more enjoyable. Initially interrupt the lungeing to offer a reward after every couple of full circles, and then gradually extend the interval.

It's showtime!
The bow and Spanish walk

Many of us dream of being able to teach our horse to do circus tricks because they are visible proof of a properly functioning communication between human and horse. Positive training makes it easier to perfect the execution of a variety of these exercises. In the following section I will describe in detail the key exercises of bowing, which in classical circus work is the foundation on which exercises such as kneeling and lying down are built, and the Spanish walk, which is used extensively when working on harder movements later in training.

The bow

In this exercise the horse makes a bow, moving backwards and upwards while supporting itself on one foreleg, or to be exact on the knee and cannon bone. When out in the field you will often see horses taking up almost the same position when they try to get to grass on the other side of the fence. You will also see similar patterns of behaviour among horses that are play-fighting.

Before you start work on the exercise prepare by giving your horse a bit of feed just above the ground directly in front of its forelegs, and then offer it again from behind and between the fore-legs to encourage it to lower its head further. This preparation should of course also be accompanied by a click and then a tit-bit.

In the next phase, and to help it along, gently lift up your horse's foreleg. You must always do this together with a clear signal so that your horse can distinguish this type of lifting from when you lift its legs to pick out its hooves. When lifting up its leg you will also need to ensure that the upper part of the foreleg stays pointing vertically down and that the cannon bone remains parallel to the ground. Only then will the horse later be able to support itself on the leg correctly, and won't try to carry all its weight just on the joint.

You should only carefully support the leg and never pull it backwards.

The movement backwards and upwards comes about through clever use of a long tit-bit such as a carrot. The horse will start to move like this by itself and you need to follow the movement along up the foreleg so that the leg remains at the same angle as at the start. If the knee comes

Once the horse has mastered the basic bowing movement the treat should be offered in front of its chest to prevent it dropping its head down between its legs.

too far back the horse will become unstable and won't be able to hold its balance, possibly swaying forwards.

Holding the bow for any length of time is only possible if the horse is balanced in the correct position. The supporting leg – the foreleg that is holding the horse's weight – should be vertical in relation to the ground, and the leg that is stretched out needs to be as straight as possible. The hind legs must not be too close together and as far back as necessary to ensure that the supporting foreleg doesn't come into contact with them. Only then can the horse round its back correctly and avoid straining it.

If these basic elements are shown, the time for which the horse stays in position can be increased by gradually delaying it standing up. It is important to watch your horse carefully and to click and offer it a treat at the point just before it is about to want to get up again. In the next phase of training you need to give the signal to stand up just before the horse wants to get up. You should never try physically to prevent your horse from standing up. You should continue to lengthen the time between treats and concentrate on getting the horse to follow the command to bow. You need to pay careful attention with these more demanding exercises that the horse doesn't overexert itself physically, for example by being worked more on one side than the other, so always practise the bow on both legs.

The Spanish walk

If your horse has learned to stretch out a leg on command when in halt, for example in response to a light touch of the whip or target stick, and can walk along next to you then you can start to combine these two movements into a Spanish walk.

Lead your horse in walk and give it the signal that it has already learned, asking it to stretch one leg forward. As soon as the leg moves forward even slightly – the height is irrelevant when starting to teach this movement – reward with a click and a treat. The horse will then stop of its own

First the horse learns to stretch its leg straight out in front at the touch of the whip.

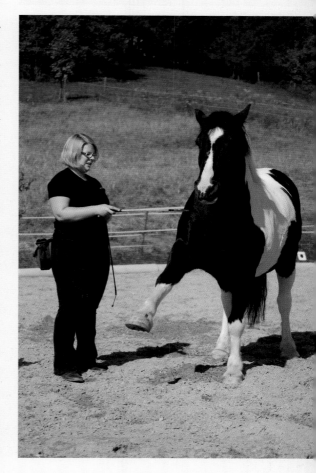

The bow should be practised on both sides to ensure that suppleness increases on both sides evenly.

accord. You must touch its leg just before the front leg is about to move forwards otherwise the signal will put the horse off its stride and out of its natural rhythm.

Repeat this with just one foreleg and gradually "raise the bar" required for it to earn its treat. At first you should reward the horse every time it stretches it leg out, then later just reward it when it lifts the leg higher to stretch it out. It is important that you never reward the horse for stretching out the wrong leg, otherwise this will cause confusion later. Parallel to this you should also work with the other foreleg so that the muscles are developed evenly on both sides and to prevent any build-up of tension.

By combining both exercises your horse will start to show a Spanish walk. Do a few steps with one leg and then the other. The first change from one leg to the other should be marked with a click and exaggerated praise. Only then can you start to change from one to the other in rhythm, and you can make it even harder by only rewarding the steps that are particularly good.

In Spanish walk rhythmical and balanced steps are more important than the height the legs are raised to when stretched. A successfully executed Spanish walk doesn't have to be particularly spectacular. The height that a horse can lift its legs evenly is dependent on its conformation and the degree to which it is able to collect.

The expression it can put into the exercise, however, has more to do with the horse's personality. The Spanish walk always looks particularly expressive when the horse is really having fun doing it and when it has found the process of learning enjoyable.

Suppling work in-hand

In order to be able to work on the lateral movements, it is essential that your horse understands the aids from the rein and hand. Closing the hand around the left rein should cause the horse to turn its head to the left and closing the right rein should result in right bend. Later you should not only be able to ask for the direction of the bend but also the degree. The horse should be able to tell, from how you hold and use the reins, whether it should do shoulder-in or travers.

For your horse to learn the aids through the reins and hands tempt its head to right and left with a treat. If it moves its head even slightly in the right direction click and give the horse a tit-bit. Increase the amount it turns the head bit by bit until you reach the desired position. You don't want to have to offer treats constantly, but to establish the signal of a hand closed around the rein, therefore start to take up a contact with the horse's mouth a few times before using a tit-bit. Gradually change to only pretending that you have a treat, until the horse reacts to the rein in the way you want. Even as you reduce using treats to ask for the bend directly, continue to use the click together with tit-bits to give positive reinforcement to the horse when it has done what you have asked.

When working in-hand it is very important that your horse has learned the signals for halt and walking on. Most horses are already

The horse can learn to interpret the rein aids with you on the ground.

used to focusing on their handler when being led, so that if you stop suddenly when leading your horse it is likely to stand still as well, purely out of habit. You can utilise this tendency by saying "halt", or your own choice of word, just before you stop. Stop, and then when the horse stops and stands reward it with a click and a tit-bit. Do exactly the same when walking on from the halt. Say "walk on", walk forwards, and click and reward the horse when it follows you. So that the horse doesn't get bored too quickly, stop in different places around the school and do it while walking different school figures such as circles or voltes.

Shoulder-in

The shoulder-in is the most basic suppling lateral movement that a horse learns when being trained in classical dressage. The horse moves sideways and forwards, flexed and bent through its body on three or four tracks, depending on the degree of difficulty.

The shoulder-in improves the contact, it develops a horse's bend and suppleness, while also making its movements smoother and preparing it for collection and straightening work later on. The horse's body is positioned almost as if it were starting a volte.

Lead your horse at walk on a light contact on the outside track. Turn in as if you are going to do a volte but instead of carrying it through, after the first step keep this

By leading a horse into a volte you can develop the shoulder-in.

position and wait for one or two steps of shoulder-in from your horse. As soon as this happens click and reward it.

The aids should come from your own posture and position. The direction that you are walking in shows your horse where to go. A gentle touch on the reins on both sides at the same time collects the horse into your hand. Looking towards the hind legs represents your signal to step sideways and taking a light feel on the inside rein positions the horse's head.

Whenever your horse offers you too much sideways movement continue on to the volte, and on completion of it try shoulder-in again. The forward impulsion stops the hind legs stepping too far past the horse's centre of gravity, and to do this movement successfully it has to step through under its centre of gravity. If the horse tries to rush, break off the exercise and do something else until it quietens. If there is not enough bend then go back to the exercise in which you asked the horse to bend left and right at halt.

If after several repetitions you are getting the beginnings of shoulder-in, which your horse enjoys doing, helped by the rewards on offer, then start to refine the movement. Start to work on a circle away from the outside track because you will get a better feel of how well the horse can perform the shoulder-in when you don't have the support of the track. The horse should now slowly start to show more steps, supported all the while by rewards. Now you can also start to work on an increased level of collection, with the hind legs coming further underneath your horse. To do this you need to coordinate the aids precisely. Combine the aids given through the reins with touching different parts of the hind legs with your whip or the target stick. The horse learns

from this the individual components of the movement. A touch on the thigh means "go more forwards", a touch to the croup means "drop the quarters and come through more", while touching the hock means "lift the leg more and put it down when I stop touching you". All this will need to have been learned and practised during shaping.

If you want to start working in trot you will need to make it clear to your horse that you want it to trot quietly and rhythmically next to you. Ask it to trot first by running off alongside your horse. If it trots a few paces with you, give a positive response. You now need actually to run less but to take larger steps, because you want your horse to stay at the required pace by itself, and when running you can't keep your hands still.

Once you have taught your horse to trot happily in-hand you can start to work on shoulder-in at trot, at the same time as you are working on improving the movement at walk. As with the other movements, you should always work on both reins evenly in shoulder-in and only work in short concentrated bursts.

How to teach your horse to load itself

Once a horse has learned to follow a target stick, or can be led with a hand target, you can incorporate additional exercises to prepare for when you want to load your horse into a trailer. You can lead your horse over different types of surface, such as wooden boards, tarpaulins or even over a bridge, providing it with its reward when it is standing on them. You can also lead it forwards and backwards through narrow gaps. In this way

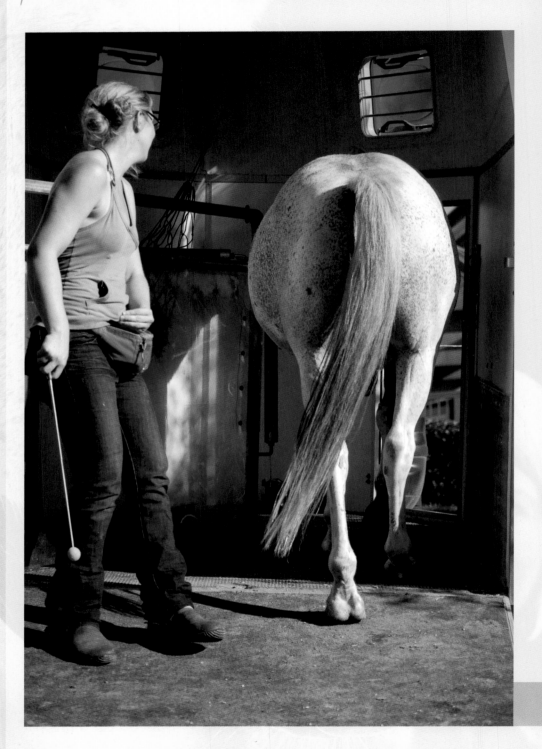

you are introducing many of the elements it will face when walking onto a trailer for the first time but in a more relaxed and playful environment.

If the horse stays relaxed throughout you can then practise with a trailer that has been checked and is securely in position. You need to allow plenty of time, and peace and quiet to practise calmly. Get the trailer ready by placing a target inside the trailer that will be used to position the horse's head, and a well-filled feed container at the front of the trailer. Lead the horse over the ramp sideways several times, using the target stick or hand target, rewarding every successful completion. If there are any signs of stress go back a step.

If this all goes well then lead the horse up the ramp and click and reward every step it takes on the ramp. Depending on the horse's previous experience, after a few steps up the ramp give the signal to back up and reward these steps in the same way. If during this session the horse walks into the trailer, mark and reward the horse when it stops at the target positioned inside. This should now become one of the horse's favourite places and a target in itself. Once the horse has recognised the inside of the trailer as being a target and somewhere it wants to go, you can start to walk alongside your horse up the ramp, and then with a suitable word such as "up" indicate that it should walk on alone to its target. When it reaches it, in other words once it is standing inside the trailer, it should get the jackpot of a filled feed bucket. After several days' practice the horse will be able to load itself happily, stand at the target and eat its feed. Then you can start to add the other elements involved in travelling in a trailer, such as putting the bar across behind the horse, putting the back up, tying up the horse and actually moving the trailer with the horse inside.

The goal of the exercise is to do away gradually with the rewards and for the horse to load with a few words of praise rather than with tit-bits. If all elements of the loading and travelling process are taught carefully and patiently using positive reinforcement, a scary trailer can be turned into one of your horses favourite places.

The aim of training your horse to load is that it should be able to walk onto your trailer happily by itself.

Riding with the use of rewards –
harmony in the saddle

Many of us ride in a particular style because we have always ridden like that, because a certain tradition demands it, or perhaps because we have a clearly defined goal such as being able to ride difficult movements. If you delve more deeply into the reasons why most people want to ride you will perhaps discover what you really feel.

A horse's movement doesn't just move its rider externally but it also moves them inside. The word "emotion" does after all come from the Latin word "motion", and so our feelings represent being moved internally. All of us express our feelings through our bodies. If you are cold you pull your shoulders up; if you are happy you may jump about. A horse's movements are directly linked with its emotions, which are expressed through its body. Given that horses are much less directly conscious of the way they are feeling, they live deep in the world of their emotions.

When riding many people want to be a part of this, and we see this as our dream. We want to experience shared enjoyment and simply feel the power and suppleness of our horses beneath us. Once we are aware that horses can only transmit the emotions that they are truly feeling when being ridden, we can understand why many a lazy, albeit comfortable, trot feels rather feeble and lacklustre. You can't expect your horse to show a positive and happy attitude when it feels absolutely no joy in being ridden. There are many ways of producing a well-trained horse, but in positive horse training riding is more like an emotional conversation. We need to help to make our horses excel and shine so that we can enjoy and share this feeling both physically and emotionally.

Horse-friendly riding

Horses can only move in a relaxed and supple fashion when they trust their riders. This trust is formed by your reactions being predictable, total concentration on what you are doing, having empathy with your horse's emotions and allowing these emotions to be expressed. A happy horse can be identified from its expression. Its ears will be in motion constantly and it takes an interest in the world about it. It enjoys its work and enjoys moving and stands up proudly. Positive horse training, focused as it is on allowing the horse emotional freedom, helps to develop the horse's personality. Horses trained using this method are more self-confident, appear to enjoy what they do, and feel well. This is an excellent basis that allows us to feel good when riding.

While we enjoy being around our horses, riding is for many of us one of the key reasons why we are involved with horses. To be at one with our horse, truly communicating with our equine partner as if dancing – all of this is inseparable from our dream of riding and owning a horse. But how often do you see a less than harmonious picture of stressed and tense horses? For the riders, too, it all seems to be far too much like hard work.

There are many levels to the conversation you may have with your horse when riding. There is the physical level, which works with a combination of balance and sensitivity, and a level of understanding that consciously recognises the connection and reflects this in dealing with the horse. There are of course certain aids that every horse can understand naturally, such as the way you shift your weight from one side to the other. A horse doesn't have to learn these laboriously. As riders we are encouraged to develop our own abilities and establish our own independent balance. Alongside this there are other types of aids, including the leg, voice and the reins. These are all signals that the horse doesn't understand subconsciously but has to be taught the meaning of actively. No young horse will, from day one, know that pressure from the legs means that it is supposed to move forwards. On the contrary, many youngsters will stand still. They have to learn these types of aid.

Horses that view being ridden as a pleasant experience will have a positive outlook on their work.

At this point, as riders we are standing at a crossroads where we have to decide which method we choose to follow. In the classical tradition the horse is generally trained to understand the rider's aids through the use of negative reinforcement. Stronger and stronger aids are applied until the horse reacts or another method of pressure, such as the use of the whip or a train-ing aid such as draw reins, is used to cause the horse to respond.

Given that horses respond to both methods (positive and negative reinforcement) I believe that we should always choose the method that is free of force and compulsion. This will also benefit your horse's mental health.

Positive emotions can change a horse's outlook

If a horse's emotional involvement in its work changes this will be reflected very quickly in the way it moves it body, and will be seen as increased muscle development. Horses that are more satisfied and happy will appear to be better trained, their topline will improve, and they will be much stronger and better equipped to carry a rider. Experiments done on human athletes have shown that fitness and muscle development are greater when the athletes enjoy their sport than when they are only going through the motions.

The outlook of horse and rider is always a reflection of the training methods used.

To give new meaning to aids that have already been learned is the first step in changing your riding style. If you praise and reward your horse whenever it does something right it will be much more motivated and attentive in its work. This can be shown in a prompt move off in walk, an energetic transition into canter, or reining back purely in response to a shift in your weight. When you are riding it is also of great help to use a clicker and to give a reward when the desired movement or behaviour has been performed. The appropriate responses to the aids will be carried out with much more enthusiasm in the future if you use this method. Your horse's outlook and expression will show you that you have chosen the right path, because it will be more inquisitive and alert. At last you have found a way of communicating your desires and needs to each other.

When you miss having a third hand

When you use training by reward while riding, you will notice very quickly that you need a particular ability to multi-task. Coordinating the individual movements and having the correct timing is not as easy as it might appear.

It is of particular advantage if you can condition the horse to respond not only to the clicker device itself, but also to your own tongue clicking or to an alternative word or sound that indicates praise. The advantage of this is that you don't have to hold the clicker in one hand but have both hands

Short reward breaks when riding help to motivate the horse and reinforce its bond with its rider.

free to hold the reins. Given that tit-bits can be stored in a saddle bag or on a bag attached to your belt, you will simply need to hold the reins in one hand and offer the treat with the other.

Granted, the start of clicker-riding will be clearly different from your usual riding lesson. The exercises will be interrupted continuously by the horse stopping and standing still to receive its regular offering of treats. It will look a bit like stop-and-go riding. For a traditionally trained rider it will take a bit of getting used to, but for your horse it will probably be the most enjoyable training session in its life. It will receive a positive response constantly, and will be praised and showered with treats.

● The horse is receiving precise information about what it has done correctly, and as a result will become more engaged with its training.

● To train effectively using a clicker the rider has to consider carefully what exactly is required from the horse in terms of its behaviour and movement, and has to learn to recognise these at the right time.

● Given that horses can only concentrate for a few minutes at a time, you will also need to take lots of short breaks.

● End each exercise when it is at its best and don't wait for it to go wrong.

● Due to the continuous supply of rewards offered when training in this way horses have an inordinate amount of fun when being ridden and this is reflected in a more positive outlook.

● By alternating the side the horse is offered its treats on from left to right, the horse will be stretched evenly and will become more supple.

● Owing to the rapid success experienced you can lengthen the sessions more quickly, and you will need to interrupt them less and less. Very soon you will produce real fluidity of movement.

Practical examples of riding by reward

Long and low – an example of shaping

It does a horse good to learn to stretch down, and it also serves to balance it after being asked for a more raised outline. The horse should round its back, allowing the head and neck to lower and the hind legs to come further underneath its body, using its stomach muscles more. This extended outline comes from the rider's seat and can be supported by using the process of shaping. First, use the clicker to mark and then reward every time the horse stretches and lowers its neck. Gradually make it more difficult by changing the criteria from rewarding the smallest of stretches to rewarding the horse only when it lowers its head and

A long and low outline can also be practised with just a neck ring and without a bridle.

neck to a defined point, such as when the mouth is level with the point of its shoulder.

After this, set further criteria such as the engagement of the quarters or the rounding of the back with the shoulders lifting. Gradually mark only the really good steps. This outline should be practised at all paces in future training sessions. In order that you don't have to interrupt the horse's flow of movement constantly you could also use the "keep going" signal detailed later on page 116.

Difficult exercises such as the turn on the haunches using only a neck ring should be practised regularly so that the horse can do them with confidence.

stood or those that they haven't performed for a long time.

Especially when being ridden, horses learn a huge variety of different aids, signals and movements, added to which there are demands for greater physical flexibility. It is only natural that now and again a horse won't perform an exercise perfectly. Whenever your horse doesn't react to an aid you need to ask yourself: "Does my horse really understand my aids? Have I trained it to respond to this precise aid or could it be confusing it with something else? Have I applied the aid as I would normally, or am I perhaps a little stiff today? Is my horse physically capable of doing what I am asking it to do? Is it sufficiently motivated? Have we practised this regularly enough recently?" It is unfair to ask a horse to do something that it can't do. As a rider you should therefore always be at pains to think about what you are doing and what you are asking of your horse, and always look to yourself for the cause of any misbehaviour or mistakes.

Horses can also forget

Can you remember the most important rules for mathematical differentiation? No? Then perhaps you know the rules for multiplying fractions? No, really? Well you are not alone. Just as we can't remember everything that we have ever learned, horses sometimes forget exercises that they have not fully under-

Teaching the riding aids – the basic principle

In training the riding aids you need to follow a specific concept that can be applied regardless of the aid.

If you want to teach the horse to do something new, you need to work initially without the use of the aids that you will teach later, but instead work just with the horse's natural reactions. An example of this is when you use your own weight

In positive horse training the rider can teach their horse the meaning of the individual aids in small steps.

to throw your horse off-balance so that it tries to regain its balance by stepping across to find its new centre of gravity. It

would make no sense to use one of the aids to be introduced later, because at this stage the horse won't know or understand the aid and won't act in the way you want it to. Instead you can either use your own weight, or ask a helper on the ground to give the signals that you taught when working in-hand to ask the horse to carry out a specific action. You can then dispense with your helper gradually and introduce the appropriate aid.

This procedure is based on the way a horse learns. The rider's aids can only be learned and understood if after a signal, in this case one of the aids, the horse displays the required behaviour or action. To clarify this, think of all the riding school horses that are being "nagged" constantly by the legs of their many inexperienced pupils. The horses will react less and less to the leg and the aid loses all of its effect. We describe this as the horse becoming dead to the leg. This is a natural process in learning behaviour. Any outside stimulus that is applied constantly to the horse, whether it is the beginner rider's unsteady hand or their constantly banging leg, will become something that is totally normal and will have no meaning for the horse or for what it does, and thus will cause no reaction. It becomes a form of background music. If you don't want to train your own horse in a similar way – remember this behaviour is not the horse's fault but caused by the rider –you should only ever apply an aid when the horse is in a position to understand it as something that will influence its own actions. In other words apply the aid when the horse understands which behaviour or action the aid is supposed to introduce.

For example, the aid for canter can only be introduced when we are already able to get the horse to canter, whether by following a more experienced horse into canter or by relying on a voice command from someone lungeing you from the ground. Only when you are certain that your horse will canter should you apply the new aid. This tells your horse that this will be the signal that you want it to canter in response to in the future. Only with correct timing in applying the aid just before the moment when it starts to canter, and then by repeating it and dispensing with the other aids used before, such as your helper's voice command, will the horse understand the meaning of the canter aid. If the horse's transition into canter is sufficiently praised often enough then the horse will willingly accept the canter aid as the signal that it should canter.

A horse thus associates our newly introduced aid with its own actions, and it then becomes the catalyst for the appropriate behaviour. It is obvious that you should always give the same aid for a specific movement, which in turn assumes a high degree of skill from the rider. At the start

To halt from canter puts great strain on the horse's joints, so the keep going signal is a good concept to introduce.

horses will find it easier if they are also given a voice command alongside the new aid because they are usually accustomed to the use of the voice command during in-hand work.

The "keep going" signal!

When riding, you often want to reward something without interrupting the exercise. If for example you are working on the canter it isn't really very sensible to click too often because the horse will have to stop cantering to receive its treat, and it could strain its joints stopping suddenly and too often. For situations such as this the introduction of the "keep going" signal can be very useful as a bridging signal. This signal becomes a tertiary reinforcement after an exercise has been established and gives notice of the secondary reinforcement, the click, and the primary reinforcement, the actual reward in the form of a treat that is to come. The keep going signal tells the hose that it is doing the right thing and to carry on and that if it does keep carrying on then it will get a reward soon, as if to say "you are almost there".

The horse stays motivated because it has high expectations of a reward and will continue to concentrate on its work. The signal to keep going also encourages the horse to work even harder.

To make the horse understand the new tertiary reinforcement it has to be conditioned in a similar way to the clicker. When riding this is best done when you are doing something simple that the horse knows well, for example cantering over a long dis-tance. While the horse is cantering, at the point when you would normally use the click that would result in the horse stopping its behaviour (cantering) you instead give the new signal, for example the word "good", or "go on". Soon after this you click as usual and give your horse its treat.

It is important in the repetitions that follow that you keep to the same order: horse performs the behaviour – keep going signal as tertiary reinforcement for a gradually extended period of time – click as the secondary reinforcement – reward with a treat as the primary reinforcement. In the training that follows the new reinforcement is introduced more and more frequently, whenever you don't want the horse to interrupt its motion. Once established the keep going signal is a very important tool for training new and complex patterns of behaviour.

Less is sometimes more

Many riders dream of being able to ride their horse just with a neck ring, or even ride without anything near its head at all and still be able to communicate. The way in which the commands or aids are dispensed with is important here. Initially you can, in the transitional stage, ride with a combination of neck ring and bridle, using the reins less and less and your weight and voice more and more. Start with the easiest of exercises and gradually try something more difficult.

> If you don't want to have to interrupt a complex movement such as renvers, the "keep going" signal will bridge the gap until the next click is given.

At the beginning stay in walk and practice stopping, walking and turning. If you want to do away with the reins totally you need to ensure that you always apply your aids in a specific order so that the voice comes first, then the weight or leg aid, and then the neck ring and only at the end the reins. If your horse stops in response to only the vocal command praise it enthusiastically.

For turning, you should also check whether the horse will respond to just your weight. If it doesn't react you can use the neck ring on the side opposite to the direction in which you want to turn, in other words use the ring to make it clear to the horse where you want to go. If the communication via the neck ring works, repeat the exercise by leaving the ring alone and concentrate totally on the remaining aids. This type of riding is naturally only sensible when you are working in a safe environment and you feel comfortable and secure yourself. It is a slow process but one that creates greater harmony and eventually makes horse and rider into a team.

Learning by reward helps to realise your dream of riding without reins.

The enjoyment of shared movement is the result of horse-friendly training.

Dr Doolittle's dream –
new horizons for our dialogue

Once we are on the new path of communication and have expanded our horizons for the conversation between human and horse we feel closer to our horse's inner being. This book makes no claim to be a collection of patented recipes. You mustn't think that the examples given here can simply be copied and will appear exactly the same in your field at home. There is no perfect solution, no step-by-step instructions that can be used with every individual horse and in every situation. But I am convinced that in this book readers will find ideas for spending time with their horses, and that they will be stimulated to try out some of the methods I have introduced and hopefully learn to value their inherent strengths.

An open and sympathetic exchange of wants and needs forms the basis for any level of communication in which human and horse can look each other in the eye. In this book I have been able to show you only a few of the basic

A true dialogue exists when each participant is sensitive to the emotion of the other.

skills for establishing a shared language with your horse, teaching you some of the important words, looking at a logical structure for comprehension and perhaps even learning some helpful phrases from what still might be a foreign language. But even if we read all of the foreign language books in existence and know all our vocabulary off by heart we still may not be able to conduct a conversation. A serious discussion with your partner isn't marked by the fact that you are speaking the same language, but rather that there is mutual interest, a curiosity about how the other is feeling inside and an equal exchange of information and emotions.

People like us, overflowing as we tend to be with ideas, should ask ourselves critically whether we really are always a pleasant conversational partner for our horse. Even in positive training there is the risk that we force communication onto our horses and often decide the topic of conversation. A trusting partnership is fed by balanced cooperation. Our horses in their natural state can teach us the art of listening and careful observation.

Does this really constitute a true dialogue? In my opinion a real dialogue exists only when each participant is sensitive to the voice of the other. Horses have a very refined instinct when it comes to sensing our emotions, they can read our body language and draw their very own conclusions from the signals we give out. The horse itself can only express itself through its body language. Our capacity to perceive our horse's feelings and adapt our own behaviour accordingly is therefore a decisive factor in how our dialogue develops.

During training, it is very important to me that horses enjoy working with their handlers and show it through their expressions. Soft eyes, an alert gaze, being relaxed around the mouth or having a curious probing top lip are all signs of this. In this book I have only selected pictures of horses that are showing the fun and enjoyment they are having with their handlers. From my point of view it is only by having a happy horse as a partner that training really makes sense.

Any feedback you get from your horse is therefore important for your dialogue. Even if the horse shows that it is feeling pain or is stressed, this is also part of your non-verbal conversation. If our horse sends us a message it is our responsibility to do our best to respond to it. For the horse the most important word in our mutual dictionary, alongside our own "yes", is the certainty that its own silent "no" will be heard by us.

In my opinion the methods introduced throughout this book are the foundation of a common language. We have learned a common vocabulary and some basics of grammar, in effect a way to combine individual words and signs, with the help of shaping or target training, to make some sort of sense. In order to move on to learn the "high school" version of this dialogue and do more advanced work with your horse you will need to refine this understanding further. It is your horse, through its own creativity, that will show you what is possible. It is capable of learning advanced concepts, new exercises and games when you allow it to do so and accompany it through the learning process. The language that you and your horse share will be unique to you. By taking the time to understand your horse you can achieve what you have dreamed of for so long.

Appendix

Acknowledgements

My heartfelt thanks go to my two- and four-legged photographic models who have been captured so beautifully by Cornelia Ranz. I would especially like to thank Alexandra, Verena, Kerstin, Marianne, Cornelia, Nadja, Sylvia, Edgar, Ute, Nina, Patricia, Stefanie, Martina, Erika, Julia, Nathalie and their horses Bessi, Gloa, Selina, Naps, Jimmy, Nora, Faroush, Dinah, Naeryo, Spark of Hope, Prinz William, Lego, Morghain, Olaela, Moirin, Doc Hollywood, Skadi, Enja, Cheri and Bernhard. Without all of you clicker training wouldn't be what it is – this method of training has only come alive as a result of your efforts and engagement.

Further reading

Thies Böttcher:
Gentle Horse Training.
Cadmos Publishing 2010.

Kurland, Alexandra:
Clicker Training for Your Horse.
Dorking: Ringpress, 2004.

Wendt, Marlitt:
How Horses Feel and Think.
Cadmos Publishing 2010.

Wendt, Marlitt:
Trust Instead of Dominance.
Cadmos Publishing 2010.

Contacting the Author

www.pferdsein.de
Marlitt Wendt's homepage with information on the themes of equine behaviour and creative training, with details of seminars and lectures.

Index

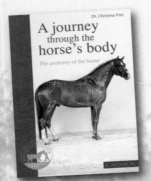

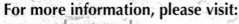